GREENER PASTURES

GREENER PASTURES

BEYOND MT. ABUSE

TINASHE LA

Disclaimer

The moral rights of Tinashe La to be identified as the author of this work have been asserted in accordance with the Copyright Act 1968.

First published in Australia 2018.

Any opinions expressed in this work are exclusively those of the author and are not necessarily the views held or endorsed by the publisher.

All rights reserved. No part of this publication may be reproduced or transmitted by any means, electronic, photocopying or otherwise, without prior written permission of the author.

All of the information, techniques, skills and concepts contained within this publication are of the nature of general comment only, and are not in any way recommended as individual advice. The intent is to offer a variety of information to provide a wider range of choices, now and in the future, recognising that we all have widely diverse circumstances and viewpoints. Should any reader choose to make use of the information herein, this is their decision, and the author and publisher/s do not assume any responsibility whatsoever, under any conditions or circumstances. The author does not take responsibility for the business, financial, personal or other success, results or fulfilment upon the readers' decision to use this information. It is recommended that readers obtain their own independent advice.

National Library of Australia Cataloguing-in-Publication entry

Beltz, Nkandu, Publisher

Author: Tinashe La

www.tinashela.com.au

Title: GREENER PASTURES BEYOND MT ABUSE

(Paperback)

ISBN: 13: 978-0-9945938-4-9

Subjects: Inspiration Anecdotes

Success Anecdotes

Self-actualisation (Psychology) in women

 A catalogue record for this book is available from the National Library of Australia

Published by AscendSmart Institute

DEDICATION

I dedicate this book to people who help in fighting domestic violence and abuse in society.

CONTENTS

A personal note from the publisher — 2

Foreword — 3

Acknowledgements — 5

Words of Acknowledgement for Tinashe La — 9

Introduction — 11

Chapter One   Reflection On My Life Pre-Australia — 13

Chapter Two   Introduction to Domestic Violence and Abuse — 31

Chapter Three   My Heart — 49

Chapter Four   Losing My Virginity — 65

Chapter Five   Embarrassment in front of the whole church — 87

Chapter Six   Life Changing Holiday — 99

Chapter Seven   Immigration Revisited — 117

Chapter Eight   Forgiveness and Freedom — 135

Chapter Nine   Categories of Violence/Abuse — 139

Chapter Ten   My new relationship — 153

Chapter Eleven   Was everything all doom and gloom? — 157

Recommended Readings — 163

About the Author — 167

A PERSONAL NOTE FROM THE PUBLISHER

To the reader,

As the founder of AscendSmart Institute, my publishing company, I make it a tradition to offer a personal review of each of the authors we publish. The reason I do so is so that you, as the reader, can gain further understanding of why this book is so important to you in your life.

Tinashe is one of the most humble and loving people I know; I was very much touched by her story, her personal power and resilience to want a positive change in her life. She has raised very important topics in this book—they are very personal, sensitive and confronting.

Reading through this book, I hope you will be inspired to make your own life choices and stand your ground. If you are going through a difficult time, speak up; even though your voice is shaking, seek help. If you know someone who is going through a tough time, please don't judge—support them and encourage them to seek help. In Botswana, we have a saying: 'Only the pot knows how hot the fire is'. You cannot feel for other people; you can sympathise with them but empathy is more important.

You are blessed to be reading this book and it is my sincere hope that you will get as much out of this book as I did.

With love and gratitude,
Nkandu Beltz

FOREWORD

Hi Tinashe La,

Congratulations on getting this manuscript going; it reads very well. This is your experience and fortunately you're one of the few willing to speak out about these issues, otherwise they mostly pass unheard. Sad as it may be, it has a happy ending; there is a sense of determination and triumph. It is a narrative that will benefit many readers. Its strength lies in its originality, as it is based on a personal experience. Your personal experience is very useful in examining these issues. You're not making a personal attack on anybody or institution, except to present the contradictions inherent in our human interactions and relations, which require clarification through serious conversations with each other. I see your work in this context. It speaks to many people, as the subject of domestic abuse is with us. There is something in there that speaks to African parenting and its insensitivity to psychological development imperatives that need to be taken into account when raising children. It is good that your writing is bringing this into focus.

You also raise concerns about the problematic nature of African cultural values which do not prepare young people to think critically when confronted with unexpected problems, such as domestic abuse. It is great that you do raise these issues because we do need a solid theoretical framework through which to construct our identities and self-knowledge. Does African culture have to ignore the knowledge generated by disciplines such as psychology, philosophy, sociology, cultural studies, anthropology and science? Your reflection on these issues is not intended to embarrass anyone; instead, you're raising fundamental questions which we need to grapple with. At what point do we disengage from traditional dogma and work towards a more adaptive cultural orientation that encourages self-realisation? How do we begin to critique these traditions which serve no enduring benefits, save for a psychological fantasy?

You have examined the hypocrisy in religious communities both in Zimbabwe and Australia; these are matters of moral concern which don't have to be left to experts to discover. Many of our young people rely on these institutions to manage themselves, morally and psychologically, and therefore they do need to come under public scrutiny. Your personal experience is very useful in examining these issues. It highlights problematic experiences that demand a collective responsibility to scrutinise, for example: is African parenting perfect? Does it prepare the young ones towards critical attitudes and creativity? Does African parenting empower girls in the same way it does boys? I am glad you started this conversation and, personally, I feel that the content in it is okay for publication.

Congratulations once again and all the best with your publication.

Don't back down to conservative and retrogressive thinking, keep moving on.

Dr Peter Mbago Wakholi

Author of *African Cultural Education and the African Youth in Western Australia: Experimenting with the Ujamaa Circle*

Unless you take the first step you will never see nor know the endless possibilities awaiting you

—Danny La

ACKNOWLEDGEMENTS

First and foremost, I would like to thank God for fulfilling His promise a few years ago. In 2012, I travelled to Sydney for a women's conference. Upon arrival at Pastor Pascasie Omari's house we went into prayer—you have to love Christian greetings. She prophesied that a time would come when I would one day write a book and that I did not need to force anything, but at the right time God would prompt me and I would know what to do. I would have never dreamt of myself becoming an author, even though I love to write. This was beyond my comprehension.

Recently, I was talking to my young brother Solomon about this book and he said, "You never know, this might not be even the book she meant, but give this your all." Solomon, thank you for your encouragement and wisdom.

During the month of October 2016, my big sister Nyasha said, "I think your book will be a blessing to young women out there, overcoming all you did. You need to pen it down, sister. Just sit and write, reminding women in the world that God has used you to be a light in the world. And because of you, just like the meaning of your beautiful name Tinashe, God is with us, for real." Nyasha Chikwekwete, if it wasn't for you I wouldn't have got the courage to do this, so thank you.

I would like to acknowledge my husband, Danny, for being such an encouragement, pushing me to get this book done and for the provisions to publish this book. You told me that even if the whole world didn't support me your shoulder was always there for me, and that even if I was disowned by my friends and family because of this book, you would always be there. I have seen your strength throughout this journey as you have stood by me—I love you more, honey.

To Peter and Sarah Wakholi, I love you so much and thank you for being part of this work. You and I know that this book is ours. You have been there through thick and thin. Every encouragement has been my source of strength. You have brought out everything inside me that I had for this book and more.

To the Serugga and Mpofu families, thank you for your support with this book. You were my only hope in a faraway country, and thank you for taking all the midnight calls, hospital visits and relentless trips you made moving up and down to come and rescue me when I needed you. Thank you so much for opening your homes so that when I was in trouble I had a bed to lie on. Your love is priceless. And thirteen years later we are still strong. Your kids were very young when I was going through the hardships and to have them all now as my younger brothers and sisters, and to know that they all look up to me, I am humbled and honoured.

Missy Trish, I could cry at how much you just embraced me. When every person left me, you were the only friend who stood and believed me. You brought joy, sassiness, naughtiness and open mindedness to my world that I never knew existed. I will love you till the end.

To my counsellor, Nicola, thank you for being my strength when I was weak. I have had all your unconditional love throughout my ordeals and you were always—and continue to be—a good listener. There was a time when I got courage and we went to see that lawyer in Subiaco. Unfortunately, the paperwork I had from the lawyer, which I had hidden under the bed mattress, was found and I got in trouble and lost all my confidence to pursue freedom, but you never gave up on me. You showed me the light.

To my counsellor, Lilo, you are the best. You listen and encourage me every week to keep going, thank you and I appreciate you.

Gladys Serugga thank you so much for the book cover, darling—who would have thought that your first assignment after completing your architecture degree would be to create a book cover for your big sister?

Acknowledgements

To my mum and dad and brothers and sisters, I hope you will be proud of me. The strength that you imparted in me as a child is evident in my life. I have fallen many times, but my persistence and hard work has paid off. It is all because of you. If I didn't have it in me I wouldn't have survived till now. As far away as you are, I know your prayers have been lifting me up. I love you all and respect you.

Kudzai Mupedzi, how we met is funny. But you have been such a great mate throughout this journey. Thank you so much for your encouragement.

Fidelis Mudimu, when you said you will always support me, that was all I needed to hear. Thank you so much for your support.

Angie Olsen, thank you for allowing me to offload every nitty gritty of my life. We all need that someone who just listens. I love you so much.

Ebro Kebe, I am very grateful to you and the work you are doing in raising awareness for domestic violence and abuse. I was encouraged by you and decided to also do my part.

Nkandu Beltz, I never knew I had it in me to just call out to people and ask for help. This was definitely a first in my life and I thank you for making this journey worthwhile. Reading your books and talking to you personally made me come out of my depression when I realised I was not alone. The hardships I was facing on this journey to publishing, you had walked the same journey. I appreciate and love you.

WORDS OF ACKNOWLEDGEMENT FOR TINASHE LA

'I admire your courage and resilience that you have come through these nasty experiences and that you are willing to share with others your story in order to raise awareness. There are many others out there who will relate to your story and I hope this can start the conversation which will bring about ways of creating change in the way we tackle these issues from the cultural perspective and breakdown the wall of silence.'

'You have raised serious and confronting issues here, which will cause some discomfort, however, that is the more reason why the story needs to be told. To be able to shed light on traditional parenting styles and the effect they have on the person's self-worth in this competitive world. It is not about blame but it is about critiquing our traditions in order to bring about dialogue towards change and prepare our youth for the globalised citizenship.' Sarah Wakholi

---

'It is a heart-daring story to write, while telling your story healing continues. From your story many will be touched and everyone checks their lives to both young and old there is a connection. It is called breaking boundaries, it is a third dimension of you. Your experience will change lives.' Pastor Timothy Serugga

INTRODUCTION

First and foremost, I am not a marketer of any social group, culture, religion or company, nor am I a qualified minister or counsellor. I am just Tinashe La, an ordinary 32-year-old, African-Australian Christian woman who survived domestic violence by the Grace of God. I am sharing my own personal story so that others can learn from it and people in the same situation can relate to what I went through, to help increase awareness of domestic violence and abuse. You might not have experienced violence or abuse, but I believe my story will offer insight into how you can help someone who is going through abuse, be it a neighbour or a friend. I am hoping to raise questions which demand serious conversations. I am not hoping to achieve any personal glory or financial gain; I just want to help bring awareness and hope. You might have been abused or in an abusive relationship, but that is not the end of you; there is still more ahead of you, it's not easy, but it is possible. If I had given up on my life the couple of times I felt that way, I would not be here today sharing my experiences.

If there is anyone who feels offended by anything written in this book, I do sincerely apologise in advance, because my story is a personal reflection with no intent whatsoever to offend anybody.

To the readers: the main reason why I have written this book is to raise awareness of domestic violence and abuse, particularly to those who are not aware of it, by sharing my own personal experiences. Many people are terrified of talking about domestic violence and abuse for many different reasons, such as personality, society, upbringing, culture or religion. People accept domestic violence as a norm and even encourage people to be silent; I was the same, which is why I can relate and understand, nevertheless, I want to be the voice of those who can't speak. Many people cannot relate or understand what a person goes through during times of abuse; having been there, I am here to hold hands with you and say I can understand you, I don't know everything but it's okay to talk about it. I am encouraging anyone who has been abused or who is in an abusive relationship to believe that there is hope for you in this world. There is a better man/woman/family out there for you, regardless of how long it takes; there is joy in abundance after abuse and there is healing for you out there. Maya Angelou once said, 'Now no one is going to make you talk—possibly no one can. But bear in mind that language is man's way of communicating with his fellow man, and it is language alone which separates him from lower animals.'

TO MY FAMILY

First and foremost, before I inscribe anything, I sincerely apologise to my parents and siblings for not having the audacity to sit down and tell you what I went through during my early years of settlement in Australia. You have known bits and pieces, but I have never told you the whole story. I had many opportunities but I did not have the confidence to share my experiences with you. I kept these things to myself. In 2011, I travelled back to Zimbabwe merely to tell you of how I had come to be the woman you saw, but again I was not bold enough. I returned to Perth a bit disappointed with myself. However, I assured myself that in God's time it shall be done. I love you all so very much and I hope you will be able to see my heart through this book.

Chapter One

Reflection On My Life Pre-Australia

Two things fill the heart with renewed and increasing awe and reverence the more often and the more steadily that they are meditated on: the starry skies above me and the moral law inside me

— Immanuel Kant

CHAPTER ONE
REFLECTION ON MY LIFE PRE-AUSTRALIA

If I am to write about my childhood, it would have to be in another book. A lot of great and positive things occurred and I am grateful to my parents for raising me to be the strong and hardworking woman I am today. Nonetheless, I am only giving a snippet of the few things that I feel moulded me to be the person who would allow a man to abuse and violate me without moving an inch.

Chapter One: Reflection On My Life Pre-Australia

I remember when I had graduated from kindergarten, we went to register for grade one. I was the youngest and I remember being told that I had to wait another year to start. I refused to wait for another year and cried because my cousin sister had been admitted and we had always done things together since we were born. I felt this was unfair and I was not having it—I threw a tantrum and ultimately got admitted with the rest of the kids. Remembering this and how I stood up for myself at the age of five, I have often pondered why I never had self-confidence growing up after that, why I never felt beautiful, why I had such low self-esteem and feared so much to speak out when I was young, as one thing is certain: I was dearly loved by my family, had a great upbringing and was never ever abused in any shape or form.

As a girl child growing up I began struggling to open up to people for fear of being misunderstood or judged, and at times I felt I could not meet the expectations placed on me. I always thought I was alone, and that no one could understand me; I struggled with this for most of my childhood. I didn't know then, because I was only a child, but I was feeding this monster—*fear*—and it grew to be too big for my boots.

Looking back, I now understand why I always befriended teachers and older people from primary to high school: because they listened. Sometimes that's all I needed, someone older out there to talk to without them putting my point of view down, and for them to say, 'I understand what you are saying'. I felt like the African culture at times did not give room for a child to debate their own point of view, even when they were right. The elders were always right, even when one knew they were terribly wrong. I am grateful that beyond the mountain of struggles I faced there was always someone who had been through the same experience as me, and it made a big difference when they acknowledged that what I was saying was right, and this kept me going.

In contrast to traditional parenting styles, I loved how the former Prime Minister of Australia, Tony Abbott spoke about his differing views with daughter Frances on the same-sex marriage debate. He said how proud he was that his daughter is an independent woman, [1]"both of us raised Francey, as our other daughters, to be her own person and I am proud of her. I am

---

[1] Greg Brown. Same- sex marriage. The Australian, Sep 19, 2017. https://www.theaustralian.com.au/...will.../1905eb94944426499ed62a2be4a260f5

proud of the fact she is an independent woman, who has her own thoughts and who does her own thing. I respectfully disagree with her on this issue but I am certainly very proud.' To me, this is a great example of mutual respect between a parent and child. We do not always have to agree on everything, but I believe everyone deserves respect and the right to say their own point of view without being intimidated and bullied.

For example, during my high school days, two couples that I was close friends with showed very visible signs of family violence and abuse. Aunty Dee, a neighbour I knew, who dearly loved me, called me to her house one day as she knew what was going on. She told me what she knew regarding the couples involved in the abusive relationship and asked me for my thoughts. Because she was so open and did not try to cover up the truth, I was also encouraged to open up to her. She told me to forgive these two couples and asked me to set a good example for all the children who were involved in this occurrence. I took Aunty Dee's words to heart and that is why I don't have any hard feelings regarding the exposure to this period of time till today as I forgave the adults involved.

Unfortunately, Aunty Dee did not have a good name in the neighbourhood and I remember getting in big trouble for associating myself with her. It truly hurt and confused me deeply, because regardless of what everyone said regarding Aunty Dee, to me she had been nothing but the best mentor in a situation where everyone else pretended and stayed quiet. I was just a child and not courageous enough to stand up for myself and Aunty Dee and so I kept quiet and did not defend my acquaintance with Aunty Dee. However, the fact that when everyone else kept quiet she reached out to me, means that I hold her dearly in my heart. No matter what society branded her, to me she was an angel. This is a lesson to many people that at times it is good to perceive someone for yourself based on your personal relationship with that person and not what others perceive.

After I finished high school, Thulani Gavhu, a friend, wrote me a farewell message. I have read this note hundreds of times and I am still in awe at how someone could describe me so perfectly. I am often encouraged by this

Chapter One: Reflection On My Life Pre-Australia

message when I am feeling down, as I remind myself that someone in high school could see great potential in me. This is what he wrote:

To begin with, it is very sad to note how time flies and we never knew that one day we would be going our separate ways for good and never to meet again in the Arts Room where our friendship began and where it is likely to end, in case we fail to see each other again in future because of so many things, including even death. It's one of those things Tinashe, but I am very sure that we are only saying goodbye for formalities' sake, I think the best words here should be 'see you soon' because I'm sure I'll be meeting you soon somewhere in Mount Pleasant before the year 2003 ends.

Let me rewind my stay with you over the past two years at Bradley. It's only a shame that I do not recall when we really started talking to each other, but during my first days at Bradley I told myself that Tinashe is a true example of the people with the tag "musalad" (meaning 'snob') on them. It was in the way you presented yourself (you still do) that made me see you as a musalad. Also, you were very quiet, a person would be afraid to converse with you thinking that you were someone really out of this world. It's only that I then managed to see the real you and I am glad that I managed to befriend you, though at first, I couldn't find the guts to talk to you. I thought you were selective, but then you proved me wrong.

It's like I enjoyed every moment I shared with you, through all the difficulties you went through and also the ones I went through. One thing that I will certainly remember you with was the way you were at times afraid to stand up for yourself to say "to hell with those who hate you for nothing". You always took things softly even though some things really got into your nerves and some were really sensitive and if all that had happened to me, I think you know very well that there would be drama. I have great respect for you for the way to dealt with all your problems with other peeps of yours. You usually remained silent and that made me realise that the saying "silence is golden" is actually true. Ben Johnson even said, "Calumnies are best answered with silence" and to a great extent, that helped you a lot. One thing for sure is that people will get tired of talking crap and nonsense if they find out their crap and nonsense is actually failing to be of any use and I am sure you saw that too.

Also, allow me to commend you for being a good girl. I never heard your name in gossips, you were usually outpaced with fresh news. You really were a nice person, always ready to offer your help in cash and kind, you were always ready to give an ear to almost everyone, including me, though at times I used to make noise with silly issues. You were at times helpful giving warnings and at times some useful information for nothing and for that I view you as a rare gem amongst thousands of useless stones in the ocean.

The other thing, Tinashe, you were too smart. I was very shy to sit next to you and most of the time I felt as if you were just being too humane not to tell me to shower like you. I'm sure your husband/boyfriend would be in deep trouble especially if he behaves like the Boukyard crew. But anyway, keep that up because Zimbabwe needs smart ladies like you. One other thing, I believe your smartness should increase your self-esteem and you should stop as early as yesterday that system of yours of always looking down upon yourself. You have great potential—more potential of success than Rambo (Headmistress).

Before I pen off, go out there and find yourself a nice man to take very good care of you and keep you happy because you deserve the best. Don't ever waste yourself because you might spoil the great future I see in you. Remember, I would like to meet your husband and possibly spend half an hour with him. I don't know why but I am sure you will notify me when you get married.

See you soon in the world and take very good care of your sweetself. Eleanor Roosevelt the wife of former American president once said, 'many people will walk in and out of your life but only friends leave footprints in your heart.' You really have managed to leave footprints in my heart and I will be hurt indeed if anything bad happens to you.

Thulani Gavhu

Chapter One: Reflection On My Life Pre-Australia

I cannot point out any particular incident that could have made me to be so quiet, reserved and fearful that people would be scared to start a conversation with me. I was always reserved at school, except when I was singing to people. However, I believe the African culture baffled me at most times and so many things never made sense to me. I read an article in the newspaper[2] and I could relate to this in so many ways

'Gender stereotypes are changing the behaviour of young girls as they feel pressured to "act a certain way". New research shows stereotypes are altering the opinions girls air, the clothes they wear, the sports and exercise they do, and how much they participate in class as a result. The Girlguiding Annual Attitudes survey reveals how girls and young women face "relentless pressure" from stereotypes on social media, TV, in films, newspapers, from peers, parents and even teachers. The survey of 1906 girls found many of those girls aged 7–10 believed "pressures of gender stereotypes" affected their ability to "say what they think".'

I can relate to this article in so many ways, and it enforces the point that it is time for changes, as this has been a problem since way back. Not much has changed unless you have open-minded guardians. I could be critiqued on my opinions as a child, but the argument I am trying to bring across is that it is at this young age that children begin to be affected by the actions of society. With every action taken, there is bound to be a reaction, whether good or bad. On my part, as I could not be outspoken, I kept everything to myself or journals.

After grade two, in 1993, I moved from the local school to a school in the city to start grade three. This was a big change from running five minutes to an all-African school (our house was just behind the school) to travelling for almost an hour to a multiracial school. From memory, a few things stood out in this particular year—my eyes were opened to so many things. On the other hand, I became very careless and misplaced a few school uniforms. After being disciplined (belted) a few times for misplacing my school uniforms, I found a way out so I could be *little miss perfect*. In the lost and found

---
[2] Young girls pressured. The West Australian. September 24, 2017.

property room there were many hats, cardigans and blazers without name tags. Out of fear, a few times I would take some of the uniforms that looked similar to what I had lost and as long as there was no name tag that had to be mine. On a few occasions, the lost and found officer in charge found out I had stolen someone else's uniform and they reported it and I felt very embarrassed. For me there was no way out and I was confused and felt out of place, so gradually I kept to myself.

I remember being disciplined occasionally for things that I had done wrong, like spending my bus fare at the school tuckshop like other kids and then asking for the bus fare from other people. As a child, I thought it was only the bad things I did and not the good that was seen, but of course the opposite was true. I was the first-born child, a girl, so the expectations and pressures to be a good role model for my younger siblings were high. However, people need to also note that in as much as it is disciplining, it affects different children in different ways and ignoring the consequences of this is not right.

After school, I was forbidden to go to other kids' houses and expected to come home straight from school, do my homework and read. So even though this was a preference on the part of my parents to have a good, quiet and well-behaved daughter, consequently our neighbours thought I was full of myself because I had moved to a city school. They thought I had elevated my status and was now a snob as I was distancing myself from their children and speaking more English. The resentment from the neighbourhood made me confused, as I could not comprehend what was going on. I could not address and tell them I was expected to stay indoors, as a result I just bottled up my frustrations and misunderstandings. Being a child and wanting to be accepted, at times I would get home and play games with the other kids whilst constantly checking the time. Later in the evening, I would rush home and wash the red soil from my feet to remove any evidence of being outside—it was literally a cat and mouse game.

In 1994, grade four, I moved schools again. I loved this school better than the previous one as I felt it was a fresh start, and eventually I finished my primary years at this school. I was quite surprised when I was made a student

Chapter One: Reflection On My Life Pre-Australia

counsellor; not only was I the tiniest compared to everyone else but I had never thought I could be a leader, of all things. I made a few friends who lived in apartments close to school, so I would walk my friends to their apartments and hang around for a few hours then go home. At times, I would find myself getting home late as I would be caught up in the late afternoon traffic rush, and I would lie and say that I had sports activities. This became a habit—lying about my whereabouts and everything else. For me, if my family did not know about it then I would not get into trouble. As a result, I grew closer to the maids that lived with us as I could be more open about everything without getting scared.

In grade five I befriended Cleo, a new girl at school who had just moved from Canada. One time she invited me to her house for a weekend sleepover. Initially I was scared to ask, but then I got the approval from one parent. So, Friday after school we went over to her house and, funny enough, she was also scared of her aunty and had not asked her, but had asked the uncle and he had approved. When the aunty came back from work she saw us playing and assumed I was just playing and would leave later in the evening. We had dinner and afterwards she asked when my parents were coming to pick me up. I told her I was sleeping over for the weekend and she disapproved because she had not been told in advance and she had not met my parents, which was fair enough.

This was late at night, and she refused to let me stay that night. It would take me two buses to go back home. I was disappointed and scared to call home and tell them what had happened in case I was never going to be allowed out again. I decided to go to my best friend's house for the weekend. I knew I was welcome there any time and when I arrived I told them what had happened and I remember telling my best friend's mum to pretend that I was not there, so that when I went home I could pretend I was coming from Cleo's place. That is how scared I was; I always wanted to be the perfect child, which I felt would please my family. Parents being parents, my best friend's mum let the cat out of the bag that I was at her place and that I had asked her to lie. You can imagine when I got home I got in trouble for cooking up such lies. There was no need for me to lie as I had done nothing wrong—I had been petrified for nothing.

The school offered many school trips for different classes, be it camping, sightseeing or hotels around the country, but I never got the chance to travel. As a child, I did not understand why other children had opportunities and I didn't. Seeing my schoolmates off on trips that I couldn't go on did not sit well with me. I would cry myself to sleep, but was never courageous enough to ask why. Eventually, I never bothered to ask for anything in particular because I thought I knew the responses in advance.

I later discovered my love for arts, and I particularly liked dancing, singing, drama and poetry, and so I would stay back for after-class activities—and I loved it. I loved sports: I played tennis, hockey, swimming, athletics and I was also a girl guide. In as much as I was involved in many things at school that I loved, looking back it was my way of being away from home as much as possible, as I felt I couldn't be myself. As I was too young to understand, to me it was a maximum-security prison, you were told what to do, where to sit, where to go and how to do it. The school would, at times, have singing and drama competitions on the weekends. Because I had allowed fear to control me, I would participate in all rehearsals during weekdays and never turn up on the day because I was terrified of asking.

As if life at home was not challenging enough for me, the religion I practised and knew little about proved even more confusing. As a child, I did not know the meaning of faith—all I could do was hear and follow instructions, but many things did not make sense and in my opinion the religion was very austere. When I conversed with the other kids about their religions and how much they enjoyed them I couldn't say the same.

From my own point of view, some of the rules and regulations had nothing to do with my faith. Not that when we asked why we could not do so many things we got a sound response, you just did as you were told. You just did not do what you were not allowed to do, period! I felt that to the adults, particularly married people, they had nothing to lose because they chose that path of their own will, but to the many young people going through adolescence, and I am speaking on behalf of other thousands of young people, the rules and regulations were impracticable. We were not allowed to do so many things,

Chapter One: Reflection On My Life Pre-Australia

including wearing jewellery, so you could not even think of piercing your ears. After I came to Australia, many times I wanted to have my ears pierced, but the fear of the unknown was nerve-racking. No matter how much people talked me into it I was terrified, until I made it a New Year's resolution to have my ears pierced at the age of thirty. I am happy to say there was nothing to be fearful of and I love it.

The religion did not allow hairstyling; we were to shave our heads and keep the hair short and natural. I reflect that there is nothing wrong with that if it is your own will and you are happy. For me, the schools I attended allowed all sorts of hairstyles, which made me so embarrassed. At the beginning of the school term, us kids would have our heads shaved; I remember crying for days after that. I and my cousin sister would be angry and upset because the hair was too short for our liking but there was nothing we could say or do.

At a young age, we started fantasising about how we wanted to grow up so quickly so we could leave our homes and go to America and be free because of what we saw on television. This affected my self-esteem from a young age. Naturally, I have big ears and they look exaggerated when my hair is very short. I was teased from left, right and centre because of my big ears by so many people, including relatives. Personally, I felt like I looked like a boy, moreover, being constantly compared to my cousin sister (who happens to be drop-dead gorgeous) did not help my self-esteem in any way.

My understanding of the religious regulations and guidelines was that relations were forbidden unless of course you were ready for marriage. Flirting with the opposite sex was not allowed. If you had a relationship with the opposite sex and were involved in flirtatious behaviour you had to confess in front of everyone and get counselling. I for one was terrified of even liking the opposite sex, as I was scared of being humiliated in front of not only my family but the whole congregation at large, which further explains my character in the years of abuse—not knowing how to behave in a relationship—as this would never have been tolerated as a point of discussion in the African culture. I did have crushes on a few boys in primary school like everyone else, but I would not have dared to take it any further. So I was shocked when I came to

Perth, when occasionally on the train ride I would see young people in school uniforms holding hands, kissing or sitting on each other's laps. Young people wouldn't dare to behave like this in Zimbabwe unless they had a death wish, even if it wasn't your immediate family disciplining you, an elder person had a right to discipline you.

Growing up, I distanced myself from male figures. Astonishingly, in the African culture, for a young girl, her uncles and grandfathers can call her their wife—that's just how it is. In my opinion, there is no issue with this, but playing *chiramo* (meaning flirting), which came with this, bothered me. At times, we would go and visit my uncles and grandfather on weekends, and they were all outspoken and fun-loving characters. When they saw me, they would open up their arms from afar and wait for me to run and get a cuddle. One incident I remember vividly, my uncle waited for me to give him a hug and he is very tall in nature, so he crouched in the middle of the road with his arms wide open and I just stood in limbo a few metres from him, looking for approval. It took a few minutes of pestering and some courage to walk over and give him a hug. Inside, I was terrified that I would be in trouble religiously for embracing a male, even though there was nothing wrong with this. Naturally, I always seek other people's approval and because it is something I have grown up with, thirty-two years later I am fighting to get rid of the habit. I am confident and know what I ought to do most times, but this weakness often causes me to delay making important decisions.

Then on the other hand, I had Uncle David, who tried to play *chiramo*. Even though the culture accepts this kind of play, personally I felt like some males were taking advantage of women. Uncle David took *chiramo* a bit seriously, and whenever he visited I would try and hide from him, but he liked me. Not only did he want to cuddle, but he wanted to kiss me on the lips with his long beard, which I found very inappropriate and disturbing. So, whenever I saw him, I was always ready to run for the hills. Then he would call after me and chase me—it was petrifying. He had a few wives and I often thought 'if I do not protect myself, I might end up being his wife'. I hated this, but because it was—and still is—the culture, I never dared to voice my concerns.

Chapter One: Reflection On My Life Pre-Australia

So, at a very young age I had already started questioning the flaws in religion, culture and traditional systems, but who would I dare to ask for help or advice when I was supposed to be quiet and minding my own business? I would quietly question why unmarried couples were prohibited to date and flirt, let alone be involved in relationships, yet most of the male elders were having affairs, committing adultery with more than one woman, and it was deemed acceptable. I felt like the young adults or youth were being over-protected, in this cacoon, but not being equipped with the right knowledge or truth about the reality of the outside world in which they would eventually have to operate and socialise. I went to boarding school for my secondary education and I remember one visiting weekend I saw how a few schoolmates did not get visits from their families. Some cried and some looked pitiful, then all of a sudden, a thought came to mind: why do parents keep having more children when they cannot care for their needs? I understand that, at times, people go through difficulties and probably there was a good reason why they could not visit, as every parent wants the best for their child. However, it is also true that some couples keep having children as they don't use contraception and as a result they cannot give proper care to their children. The sadness I saw in my fellow pupils touched me; I could see how much they were affected. Something stirred inside of me, so that when I went home for vacation I told my mother that she should not have more children, otherwise I would be disappointed. Who was I to tell my own mother about how many children she could or not have, right? Reflecting on my comments to my mother, I was not being disrespectful but I was concerned with what I was seeing and learning. I suppose this shows I was thinking critically and maturing. We are conditioned to be strong and understanding, but it is these very little things that no one talks about that affect us emotionally, socially and mentally. That is why I like having the freedom to ask when I do not know or understand and not be shut down because I am a child.

Anyway, as for me, staying away from males continued to high school and I was teased by boys. One time, a guy who was pursuing me said, 'You go on acting like you have a golden vagina, there is nothing special about you after all.' This really hurt me and I had never thought of myself as beautiful, so I could not understand where he was coming from. All I remember was being teased for having big ears; *wemazheve*, they would say in my language—big nose and skinny. My cousin sister and I would always tell people we were twins and people believed us because we had so many facial similarities, despite being totally opposite in skin tone. On the other hand, she is naturally gorgeous and I was always compared to her, which did not boost my confidence as a young girl growing up.

However, as many guys pursued me in high school, I started questioning if perhaps I was beautiful or cute, which shouldn't have been the case; I should have been happy with the way I looked and carried myself without seeking other people's approval. The only thing I was confident about was being neat—I am obsessed with cleanliness and singing. I have never thought of myself as a singer, but all I know is I can't be quiet, singing soothes my soul. The more I sang, schoolmates would join in or ask me to sing for them privately, which I happily did. There were a few people who could really sing in my eyes anyway, and whenever they made a comment about how good I sang, I never believed it. To me, they were better and I was not good enough.

Then, when I was in form three, I met Fuzzy. We slept next to each other in boarding school, and before we knew it, we were best friends. As far as class is concerned (whatever that means), I was from a middle-class family and she was from a high-class family. She loved makeup; one day, she put makeup on me and eventually she ended up buying me my first makeup kit. She used to put styling gel in her short hair, which was 'being naughty' as this was not allowed in school. We all had to have short natural hair in secondary school. And then I experimented with the styling gel and realised that it made my short hair look good (people thought I had put chemicals in it) and with some makeup on I could see a beauty in myself. She showered me with lots of love, affection and compliments, so that I began to feel different about myself. She would constantly write and draw how she felt about me and why she loved me so much. She boosted my confidence so that I felt like a million-dollar chick. She complimented my singing and gave me the nickname *tweet bird*, which is what most people know me as today.

With my new-found confidence, I ended up befriending many guys. I enjoyed the attention, knowing that many guys wanted to date me but we could not

Chapter One: Reflection On My Life Pre-Australia

go any further. With guys, when I was growing up, the more you played hard to get, the more they pursued you. During the school holidays, I was forever on the phone talking to so many guy friends, and people at home were not pleased. We had two hand phones in the house and I remember one day being questioned about a guy who was ringing from Victoria Falls. According to the elders, this guy could not have been calling a girl in Harare unless there was something going on. On my part, I could not understand why they were displeased and I was upset, because he was merely a good friend who had my back at all times. I was abiding with the rules by not dating but just talking to these friends on the phone. What more could I do over the phone?

Eventually, Loverboy pursued me and, before I knew it, we were dating. In as much as it would be of concern at that age, I didn't know love at all; he was a few years older than me and way more mature. I told Loverboy of the strict rules in my life and he was very understanding and kept his distance. Because of his understanding and maturity, I thought all men were the same—if you say *no*, it means *no*. I respected him because we could meet occasionally and he made sure I would not get in trouble. We were all on the same page, if I said no to something that was it, there was no force.

As I was in boarding school I never saw much of him, as during school holidays I always had extra lessons away from home and worked at a shop our family owned at Howard, so we hardly saw each other. We had a beautiful relationship—or rather, friendship—for four years and he was happy to wait until I finished high school to take things further, which worked for me *1000%*. We communicated through letters and we had a mutual understanding.

As old people say, there is nothing that stays hidden forever; on the first school visiting during the final year of high school Loverboy came to visit me and I had a few minutes to spare before we had to go for the afternoon study. After a few minutes, I went to the study. I thought he had left, and I had been called by the teacher on duty to go to the headmistress's office. Our headmistress's nickname was Rambo, so you can imagine she was not one to be joked with. As I walked through the office, there he was sitting in the corridor. I almost collapsed. We just looked at each other with no words spoken. I knocked on the door of the head's office and I was sweating and shaking like a leaf. I was sat down and a few teachers were in the room. I remember them asking about who he was, why he was in my room, and why he brought so much food for me and a few silly questions. These were older and wiser people so I assumed they knew, or maybe not.

A few rumours started around the school but because I was a very reserved person, there was no one who could dare confront me on what had happened that particular Saturday. The term could not go any faster; I was scared of going home because I did not know what the head had told my family. That is the first time I ever thought of drinking poison and killing myself. How was I going to explain at home? I could continue to lie that it was my aunt's boyfriend but I knew my family were not that stupid. We had communicated through letters during the term and I told him of how terrified I was of going home, and he assured me that if the worst came to the worst he would take responsibility and marry me. That was even more terrifying, marriage at that age—I could not think of anything worse. Suicide was the only solution in my mind. When school finished for the term, I opened my school report and found that I had passed all my subjects (thank the heavens!), but the head's comment read: 'Tinashe's way of conduct leaves a lot to be desired'. I didn't even know what that meant so I decided to go home and test the waters. When I got home I was told by everyone to prepare for a good beating from the elders when they returned from work and I just kept to myself, running through different scenarios in my coconut. I am happy to say nothing happened, just a few words, yet I could have lost my life for fear of nothing.

As soon as I finished high school I was on a crash programme preparing to travel overseas. I did not even know where Australia was on a map, let alone what it looked like. I had no time to discuss with Loverboy what would happen or what was happening. Funnily enough, his friends and relatives were pressuring him to get married before I left and so he asked for my hand in marriage, but I refused as I felt that I was too young to even think of such a step. After that our relationship just went downhill, as there was no certainty for the future. The day I left, he went out of town as he was upset. And that was the last I ever saw him.

Chapter One: Reflection On My Life Pre-Australia

As I reflect, I did not have the best communication skills growing up. There was no open conversation about what was happening in my life as I became of age. Writing made it easier for me as I could not see the reactions on people's faces; I didn't have to argue my case and I had the freedom to express myself to the fullest. As I feared letting people down, even if it was at my expense, I had decided it was better to suffer in silence than to voice my concerns. Unfortunately, as I matured it became hard—and it still is hard—for me to speak confidently. This spirit of fear is actually crippling: many a time it has made me, an able person, disabled.

One area that the African culture, conservative or traditional parents, and many other cultures are lacking in is the discussion of issues of sexuality with a teenager. This is totally out of the picture, especially for girls; but is this not ignoring science and psychology? When you become a teenager, is it not normal to start having hormonal changes? Why are some cultures and religious groups still ignorant and practice female genital mutilation (FGM) is a mystery. *Astonishingly,* '[3]Africa has the greatest amount of FGM, as the World Health Organization believes that somewhere between 100 million and 140 million women and girls have undergone the surgery throughout the world. 92 million of them are over the age of ten and living in Africa'. Whatever the supposed reasons are, be they maintaining virginity for marriage or eliminating sexual desires, no one talks of the problems that are caused by these acts.

[4]"What Are the Problems? There are many physical and psychological problems that a woman may face after having any of the three types of Female Genital Mutilation. These include the transmission of HIV, as the same unsanitary tools (such as unclean shards of glass, razor blades, etc.) are used to perform the surgery on many different women without being sanitised. The surgery is often performed without anaesthesia, leaving the woman in an extreme amount of pain. Women can experience extreme blood loss which can lead to possible death, as well as high infection rates, pregnancy conflicts

---

[3] Christine O. FGM: The fight for female reproductive rights for girls in developing and developed countries. 28 August 2017. http://imowblog.blogspot.com.au/2012/10/
[4] Unknown Name. Female Genital Mutilation: History and Facts. 28 August 2017. https://www.mtholyoke.edu/~mcbri20s/classweb/worldpolitics/page1.html

and psychological damage among many other things. A report states that 1/3 of the Sudanese girls who undergo the surgery do not survive it. The pain a woman goes through after her surgery is sometimes referred to as the "three feminine sorrows". Not only does the woman feel extreme pain on the day of her surgery, but she also will on the night of her marriage when her vagina is reopened, and the day she gives birth. The surgery has lasting effects for a woman.

When I compare African culture to the Australian culture, Australian parents know who you are dating (actually, they want to know and meet the person), they want to know where you are going and most parents talk about contraception, because knowledge is power. On the contrary, most African children date in secrecy because it is forbidden. Realistically, not every child is going to abstain from sex before marriage—that would be mere ignorance. When is the African culture and many other religious groups around the world going to wake up and smell the coffee, so that the young ones can be educated on preventing unforeseen circumstances?

Chapter Two

Introduction to Domestic Violence and Abuse

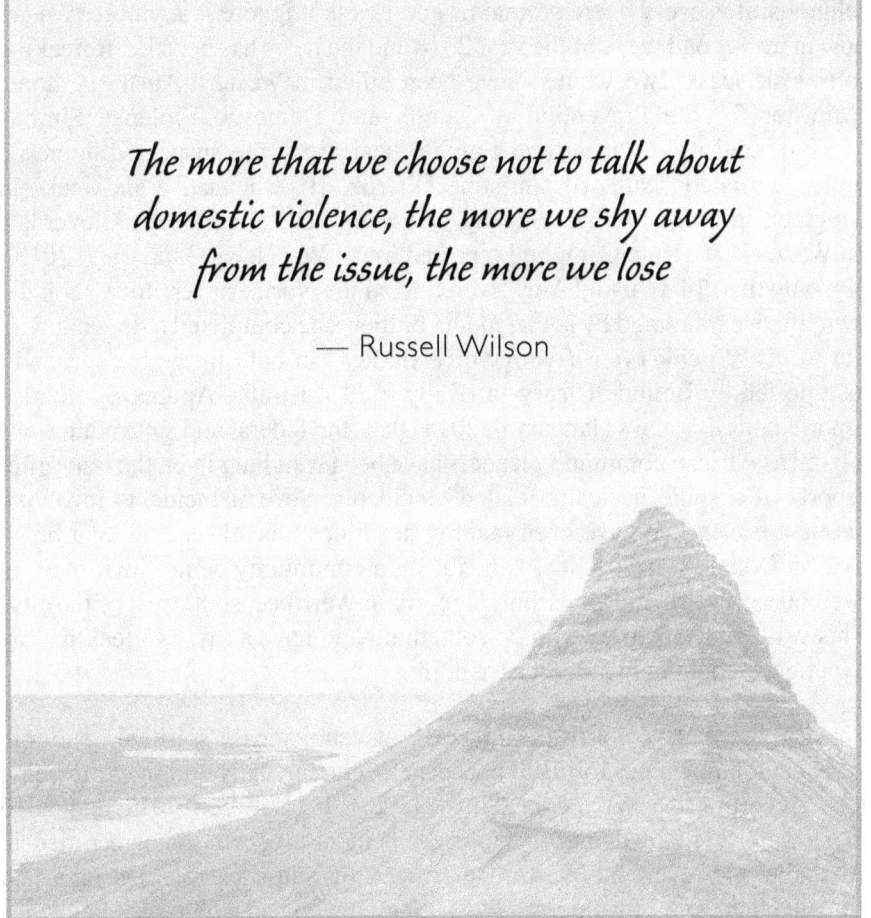

The more that we choose not to talk about domestic violence, the more we shy away from the issue, the more we lose

— Russell Wilson

CHAPTER TWO

INTRODUCTION TO DOMESTIC VIOLENCE AND ABUSE

Domestic violence and abuse have taken their place in our homes, society and religions; it is everywhere around us and I cannot ignore it anymore. We are now in the second week of the year 2018 and the news has been heartbreaking to say the least. Two women have been killed in Western Australia alone: 'Minister for the Prevention of Family and Domestic Violence Simone McGurk said it was "heartbreaking" to hear about the suspected domestic violence-related deaths of Christine D'Cruz, 19, who had a six-week-old daughter, in Mandurah last Sunday, and Margaret Indich, 38, in Cloverdale on Wednesday', Kate Campbell reported in the WA News (January 7, 2018). Not only that, 14-year-old Amy Everett from the Northern Territory 'took her own life overwhelmed by social media bullies, she completed a drawing with the words **"Speak even if your voice shakes"** in bold in the background', as reported by Belinda Cleary for Daily Mail Australia. Andrea Booth also reported on SBS news (January 4, 2018) that 'the federal and state authorities as well as African community leaders have been weighing in on the issue after reports of a spike in "gang-related" incidents. Several incidents involving young African men have been making headlines recently including a brawl at a McDonald's in St Kilda, vandalising a community centre in Tarneit, in Melbourne's west, and an Airbnb property in Werribee, southwest of the city.' This stirs my heart to want to do something and have a say, as I feel that my experience could help at least save a life.

Physical, sexual, emotional, financial, psychological, spiritual, cultural, verbal and many other forms of abuse are occurring daily and lives are being lost. According to Wikipedia (July 27, 2017), 'Between 2014 and 2016 there were 264,028 domestic violence incidents reported and recorded in Australia. However, the Australian Bureau of Statistics released data that revealed that 80% of women and 95% of men who had experienced violence

Chapter Two: Introduction to Domestic Violence and Abuse

from a current partner never contacted the police. The most common reason for not reporting was cited as fear of revenge or further violence from the current partner.' Having experienced violence and abuse from a boyfriend and surviving it, I hope to prompt further conversation around these issues. I am hopeful that people will learn something from my personal experiences of violence and abuse and the subsequent triumph.

Lately, I have been involving myself with youth and I realise that they all want to talk and discuss issues that are affecting them but which are not spoken about in their homes, circles or churches. This has stirred me more because when I was younger, I had a voice that was unknown to people around me. To most of them I was very quiet, reserved and shy. But when I was given the opportunity to speak my mind people would say I was confident and not quiet after all. Many people have no voice for many different reasons, be their personality, upbringing, culture or religion. I was the same before, that is why I can relate and understand; nevertheless, it is time to change and start encouraging people to talk about issues affecting them. Personally, I didn't know who I was then but I know who I am now. Had I talked about my struggles I wouldn't have suffered for as long as I did.

Sindiwe Magona pushed me further to even want to help more when I came across her writings, in her book entitled *Forced to Grow*, she wrote 'This organization opened my eyes to prevailing social ills. Not to anything I had not seen or known existed, but now for the first time, through discussion and action by members, I began to see myself as someone who could do something out there—away from family, job, neighbour or friend. Lending a hand was not a foreign concept to me. No. What was, was that hand could be mine, that I had the right and, indeed, the obligation to intervene in situations of distress. Other people's distress. Perhaps it had not occurred to me that I had anything to offer. In this respect, the National Council of African Women taught me I was grown up. I could assume social responsibility. People's burdens could be eased, if only I lifted a finger. And having woken up to my social duty, I inflicted it on everyone who could not escape my new-found, zestful enthusiasm.'

This book is intended to be an eye-opener, particularly for the youth and young adults, so that they may know and understand that a good relationship is not what we see on reality shows, social media and magazines. There is more to dating than just holding hands, candlelit dinners, sex and walks to the park or beach. I also believe my book will raise awareness among parents to look out for signs of whether their young ones are in abusive relationships—open communication with children is the key. Such communication between parents and children ought to be mutually respectful. As observed by an article entitled *Facts and Figures on understanding violence*, 'violence towards women is a significant and yet preventable problem. However, prevention of violence against women needs understanding of it'.

My book is also intended to sensitise abusive men who take women for granted and help them to acknowledge that their negative treatment of vulnerable women is not acceptable. I want the abusers to know that they are not disciplining a person using violence but they are actually killing them emotionally and mentally. I was beaten so many times. Those memories of pain are long gone, however, the way I think and react to situations still shows a woman in progress. For example, as a young girl I loved babies so much that anyone with a newborn knew that I could babysit without any problem whatsoever. I would get teased that I might not have children of my own because of the way I loved babies, I would go to the extent of doing my chores with a teddy bear on my back. To my shock, after my experience in an abusive relationship, I could not hold newborn babies anymore and was petrified of anything to do with babies or childbirth but I am now getting better. To any abuser, I would ask you to imagine if it was another person abusing your very own daughter, mother or sister, how would you feel? I have come to the understanding that some people have not been taught right or have not had great role models, as a result they know no different. However, I am hoping that this book uplifts men, women, the young and old to overcome life's discouragements and go on to live beautiful lives.

Just because you or a loved one have unfortunately been—or are currently—involved in an abusive relationship does not mean that is the end of your world or theirs. I am sharing my testimony to encourage anyone who has been abused to believe that there is a place and hope for you in this lifetime,

Chapter Two: Introduction to Domestic Violence and Abuse

and suicide or revenge is not the solution. There is a possibility of a greener pasture beyond an abusive relationship if you seek all the help necessary. As difficult as it is to forgive someone who has hurt you and taken away your innocence and self-worth, I found that forgiveness is the best medicine to recover from abuse. Not only is forgiveness a form of therapy to you, but also to your future and the generation to come. There is a better man/woman/family out there for you, regardless of how long it takes; there is joy in abundance after abuse and there is healing for you out there.

It's my heart's desire to inspire people; but you will not change the minds of those that have abused you, nor can you force an apology from them or those who have misunderstood you, those who have blamed you of the experiences you have faced, those who have denied your existence or life. It only takes Grace. There are other people out there who can stand in the gap of the few that have rejected you. As a Christian, my writing draws inspiration from the scriptures.

Many have not lived to tell their stories but I want to take this opportunity that I have been given to inspire someone, even if it is only one person. I want to encourage someone out there and let them know that it is not too late to leave an abusive relationship. You are not too broken to live joyfully again—those nightmares can actually go away and yes, you can sleep peacefully again. It is absolutely possible to have a life after trauma, as there is hope for you in this world. All it needs is for you to open your mouth or lift a finger and ask for help. Martin Luther King Jr. said, 'Faith is taking the first step even when you don't see the whole staircase.'

A year after high school, I got involved in a relationship with Saul from 25th December 2004 to January 2008 with the dream of getting to know him more as I progressed through my studies and subsequently getting married to him. Because of my upbringing I did not get involved in casual relationship; marriage was the ultimate goal when entering a relationship. Life turned around and in those three years with the man I called my *boyfriend*, I lived a life of fear and isolation, and suffered physical and verbal abuse, mental torture and, at times, sexual abuse.

For the past 13 years that I have been in Australia I have read, listened to stories, and seen and mingled with abused women and men, but it never occurred to me that I was one of the statistics. Not because I had forgotten my past, but I think I was just ignorant and fearful of people knowing what I had been through and their reaction to my experiences. I was comfortable with one-on-one talks but not speaking out publicly about domestic violence and abuse.

And since then I have observed, witnessed and been surrounded by women—and, at times, men—that are in abusive relationships. I have even stayed with friends in abusive relationships and I remember that the first time this occurred I had a moment of revelation—a taste of my own medicine. A person may be aware that they are being abused, but others are not necessarily aware. I have changed the way I think and have become more open about these issues, and therefore willing to share my story. I offer my support to all who have approached me. I also offer my listening ear to their plight. I am a living testimony because the families I related with were able to listen to my cry for help. I am reading the book *I have the power* by Nkandu Beltz and she emphasises *Ubuntu*, which means 'I am what I am because of who we are'. I want to be a leader to anyone suffering: if I could survive near death misses, you can too; if you are still alive, carry on living a better life.

My close friends and associates remind me of my life journey; I have come to acknowledge that I am a proud survivor of domestic violence and abuse. I want to hold hands with anyone going through abuse and encourage them to look beyond that high mountain, because beyond it are greener pastures they need to experience. A scripture from the book of 1 Corinthians 9:22 reads 'to the weak I became as weak, that I might win the weak, I have become all things to all men that I might by all means save some. Now I do this for the gospels' sake, that I may be partaker of it with you.' I make this offering to those who feel weak and hopeful in the hope that it might save a life going through hardship and misery.

Fast forward to 2018, and I am the most joyful woman you will meet, full of life, forgiveness, praise and love. Sometimes, I am overwhelmed by the love

Chapter Two: Introduction to Domestic Violence and Abuse

around me, so much so that I feel intoxicated; many a time I cry because of joy. There is absolutely no trace of trauma, or smell of smoke from the fire that once burned and I give all the Glory to God. I recently watched a Korean drama, *Secret Garden*, and came across these beautiful words: 'live while receiving love as much as you humbled yourself, as much as you have shed tears. Now live while receiving love'.

Writing this book has been hard because I am visiting places that are non-existent in my life now. That is why I believe this book will encourage all the abused out there to believe that there is more to life than what you are sacrificing yourself for now with this abuser. To the young ones, life is what you make it. You only imprison yourself as long as you keep to yourself; seek help—the sooner the better.

I grew up in a patriarchal African culture, with rigid religion, a strict upbringing and a society that most times made me feel as though I was imprisoned by my surroundings. Being a girl child made it worse. Regardless, these surroundings brought a safe cushion because as long as I followed what was expected of me I was secure. I am forever grateful that this prepared me with good human values in how I relate and respect other people. Personally, I feel that I was prepared to be a good person, hard worker and wife, to take care of my husband, children and extended families. This is all good and important, however, all these aspects did not quite prepare me for how to deal with an abusive relationship.

When I was growing up, wife beating was no big deal and people talked about it as if it were nothing. I remember three to four years ago an elder was visiting from Zimbabwe and in conversing she mentioned if she had helped one of her in-laws, her husband would beat her. I was upset because this was just a normal conversation and to her it was obviously okay to be beaten. In most cases the women I knew who were in abusive relationships never told anyone, probably out of embarrassment, shame and (surprisingly) a desire to protect their partners. I never heard of anyone being reported to the police for assaulting their partners—all I heard was either he or she deserved it. The women who received help are the ones who confessed to their negative relationships, and if their relatives had the courage to confront the abuser then something would be said and done. Other than that, it was normal to see and hear of domestic violence and abuse.

In the extended family structure I grew up in, the elders expected the girl child to dress decently by covering her whole body with loose fitting clothes, sitting on the floor with her legs crossed, covered up—not on chairs or benches. It was expected that they be well mannered and well behaved, never outspoken. Back then I had a voice, they were so many things I wanted to say or ask, but I was always told not to interrupt elders when they were speaking. The elders always ate meals separately from the children so there was never a room for open communication. When I arrived in Australia, the first culture shock I had was seeing a family (parents, the children and visitors) sitting together and eating at the dining table. I saw families sitting together in the lounge and conversing whilst they all sat on the couches. I saw how people bonded and opened up to one another, which was beautiful. I had never seen anything like this in my whole life.

Looking back at growing up, and now the dynamics of globalisation and integrated societies, it's more difficult to find the appropriate communication tools for identifying abusive relationships. As people of different racial, religious and ethnic groups come together in relationships they bring different perspectives. Whilst in my culture beating a wife was tolerated and what happened in the bedroom stayed there, when I came to Australia I realised that it is not acceptable. Even though I felt violated, and was encouraged by my new society to speak up, my cultural socialisation and upbringing kept me trapped in fear of voicing out my feelings.

Growing up, there was no alcohol consumption in the household and so it was difficult for me to relate to a boyfriend who liked his alcohol. I had seen a few people abuse others when drunk and I had also seen people who are still lovely even when they are drinking or drunk. So I didn't know what to do with a drunkard boyfriend—even the way I spoke to him when he was drunk infuriated him.

Chapter Two: Introduction to Domestic Violence and Abuse

It is my aspiration that this book can encourage young people, especially those who are in the dating stage, to be bold enough to stand their ground when a relationship does not feel right. When something doesn't feel right talk about it or ask about it and even google it. I will give more examples on the African culture as I can relate more and I know there are many similar cultures which can relate too. My plea to the young women is that once you are slapped, punched, smacked or forcefully pushed for the first time, that is it—leave him and walk away with grace. The book of Matthew 5:37 says 'But let your "Yes" be "Yes" and your "No", "No", for whatever is more than these is from the evil one.'

In my case I needed to trust my instincts; the inner voice was right, but instead I procrastinated *for way too long*. There was a time in my high school days when I was exposed to abuse behind closed doors. I heard and saw everything with my very own eyes and ears to the extent of helping clean the wounds of the abused with a warm towel. I helped clean, with tears flowing down my cheeks, and when I left the bathroom I went and cried it all out where no one could see me. I was helpless and, being a child, I was petrified of even confronting the abuser in case he hit me too. Not that the abused had done anything wrong from my own perspective, but the abuser was using assault to be dominant and show his masculinity in that house. In my culture, polygamy is accepted; a man can have as many wives and girlfriends as he likes because 'he is the head of the house', even when it is at the expense of his immediate family.

In Zimbabwe, people have accepted this terrible behaviour to the extent of giving the other women the name *small house*. I find it hilarious that people can confidently talk about *small houses* as if it were a good thing. This is another woman breaking up a relationship, marriage, family and much more. How then is it small, when someone is cheating on their spouse? How can this be a small house when AIDS (Acquired Immune Deficiency Syndrome) has killed so many people? Even though the wives might not accept polygamy, the women have no say in these issues, because it is the men who pay a dowry.

Personally, I feel that a dowry is a legitimising instrument for the insubordination of African women. The husbands do not need their wife's approval to have more women. The woman I saw being abused was just voicing her concerns and frustrations to the husband, who had not only taken one extra woman but an extra two. I saw the injustice of cultural tradition at play. This woman was working hard for her family, including the husband (who was then jobless), yet the husband was taking away everything she had worked hard for to sustain two extra women and their children—it was outrageous! I cannot even put myself in her shoes. Not only did she have to accept two other women, but she also had to support them and their children. Yet the abuser thought he had the right—after all, he had paid the dowry and he was the head of the household. What was happening behind these closed doors was never discussed anywhere, as far as I remember.

I saw this woman's courage and strength as she continued to work even harder for her children. I believe she did all of this for the sake of her children; they were all young, and African women will not abandon their children to the hands of another woman (*small house*). This is how I saw everything from the outside and I strongly believe this period in my life shaped me to be who I was during the three years I suffered abuse. I was trying to be strong; I kept everything closed in my heart and copied the strong woman, whom I had seen suffer without giving up. It's unfortunate that until today, I have never addressed this incident with the abuser and the abused, which brings me to what Scott Shaper, a former police officer, said:[1] 'Domestic violence goes way beyond just the two-immediate people involved. Look into a child's face that sees this violence every day. Then go visit that child about 10 to 15 years later and see what they have become. If they are male, they will most likely become domestic abusers themselves. If they are female they will most likely become domestic victims themselves. Why? Learned behaviour; this was their environment growing up, and to them, this is just acceptable behavior that people do. It takes a very strong person to come out of that type of environment and not have it become part of their adult lives. A child who lives with domestic violence will never forget it.'

---

[1] Scott Shaper. Domestic Violence: The Fact behind the Myths. August 28, 2017. https://www.blueribbonproject.org/our-programs/backpacks-of-love/about-backpacks-of-love/22-relationships/165-domestic-violence-the-fact-behind-the-myths.html

Chapter Two: Introduction to Domestic Violence and Abuse

The young, like me, who experience this season of abuse, are never asked how we are feeling. Being a child did not mean I had no eyes, ears, feelings or emotions. I just pretended all was perfect because I was scared and, until today, it has never been a topic of discussion. Do I have unanswered questions? Do I deserve an apology? *YES*. But in my culture, and as a child, why would I deserve this? I confided in a cousin, as this was too much to bear and, little did I know, she was also suffering in her own life. We were confused little cockroaches. Unfortunately for me, I went even quieter, probably into depression, though I wouldn't have known what it was then; my cousin took to alcohol to find solace. I saw the unjustness of culture in not helping the children in times of difficulty. Mental illness is not talked about much in the African community; most problems are associated with witchcraft, and this needs to change.

Because of my cousin's drinking behaviour, she received a beating that I will never forget for the rest of my life. I could not look at her twice, it was so horrible—even the thought of it now gives me goose bumps. I get that she was too young to be drinking, but neither did she deserve this kind of discipline. If it was a boy at that same age, I don't think they would have received the same discipline, which brings me to question whether the traditional parenting style empowers girls in the same way it does boys. My cousin was confused and needed counselling, which was not there. Like me, she has unanswered questions and absolutely deserves an apology. This is something I hope parents will begin to understand: that children have feelings and emotions too. Most African parents instil fear in their children using the term 'I will beat you'. My cousin and I were seventeen years of age when she received this beating in Zimbabwe. At seventeen, guardians should not be threatening and intimidating the young using beating as a form of discipline. At this age, a person needs a conversation, not a beating. A scripture in Colossians 3:21 says, 'Fathers, do not provoke your children, lest they become discouraged.'

The Duchess of Cambridge, Kate, recently urged parents to teach their children how to be open about their feelings and said,[2]"as parents, we all

---

[2] Bianca London. From one mother to another: Kate makes first appearance since her pregnancy announcement as she urges parents to teach their children how to be open about their feelings. September 19, 2017. http://www.dailymail.co.uk/femail/article-4895684/Duchess-Cambridge-stars-candid-video-message.html#ixzz56NWiiSAw

want our children to have the best possible start in life. Encouraging children to understand and be open about their feelings can give them the skills to cope with the ups and downs that life will throw at them as they grow up. It's important that our children understand that emotions are normal, and that they have the confidence to ask for help if they are struggling. This is why I am proud to support the *You're never too young to talk mental health* campaign by the Anna Freud National Centre for Children and Families, which is being rolled out across primary schools this autumn. The campaign's resources are excellent tools to support parents. They demonstrate how we can help children express their feelings, respond appropriately, and prevent small problems from snowballing into bigger ones."

I was recently questioned on how at grade three I could have started bottling up emotions. From what I know now, I probably suffered from anxiety and depression, but didn't even know this. I realised I could not speak freely and be understood, and found solace in writing journals; even as I grew older, I wrote more to my friends than speaking. When I see what young children are going through today, be it bullying, intimidation or abuse, I can relate. I believe parents need to start investing in the emotional needs of their children and pay more attention to detail. I hear of many eight- or nine-year-old children committing suicide nowadays and the parents cannot understand why. I was catching up with one of my friends the other day and she mentioned that the Ethiopian community in Perth, this year alone, has lost three young people to suicide. Parents are asking why. From my conversations, most African youth are terrified of their parents and guardians more than anything else. Parents misuse the words 'I will beat you', so that most children fear speaking out, even in times that they should. Irrespective of how much we all love our different cultures, I believe culture should start in the home before pleasing the extended communities.

Unlike the married woman I discussed earlier on, mine was a boyfriend relationship, and yet I tried to protect the relationship passionately. The reason goes back to my culture: we respect men as the head of the house so much, that even when they walk all over women, they still expect to be

Chapter Two: Introduction to Domestic Violence and Abuse

respected. An abuser who values their relationship should take the initiative to seek help by approaching doctors or counsellors, self-reflecting, learning from their mistakes, addressing their problems and allowing it be confirmed that they have changed. It is the abuser who needs to take responsibility, not the victim—then maybe the relationship can be rekindled without worry. I, on the other hand, took the initiative to seek help. I would run away for a few days or weeks, let him cool off and come back as if nothing had happened. This did not help me in any way; instead, it prolonged my suffering. The fact that I gave him time by going away, but he was the same when I returned, means that he was not the right man for me.

I remember that after every fight he would either cry, apologise, or use alcohol or anger as an excuse. I can only advise that once they have had the audacity to hit you, sexually abuse you or scream at you, and you do nothing about it, it becomes a vicious cycle. He never acknowledged his weaknesses in the dating stage, yet I thought he would likely change when we were married. In my culture, men pay dowry for the women. Now, I think that if he had married me and paid dowry, he would have been beaten me mercilessly—after all, he thought he owned me.

To those who still practise the customary law of dowry, I plea to the men not to intimidate and abuse women in the name of ownership. Regrettably, some men think that because of the fact that they paid a dowry, they have ownership over women. I have so many friends and relatives who are disadvantaged in their relationships because in an argument or when they disagree with their spouses they are harassed and told, 'I paid dowry for you and you should respect me as the head.' Mahatma Gandhi once said, 'Be the change that you wish to see in the world.' Personally, I love certain things about my African culture and tradition, however, in this modern age, I truly believe the notion of dowry should be critiqued and deconstructed, as it is a human creation which leads to the disempowerment of African women. Many women are abused or dying in the name of 'dowry'. As mentioned by the World Health Organisation (WHO) Geneva, 2005: 'Each culture has its sayings and songs about the importance of home, and the comfort and security to be found there. Yet for many women, home is a place of pain and humiliation ... violence against women by their male partner is common, widespread and far-reaching in its impact. For too long hidden behind closed doors and avoided in public disclosure, such violence can no longer be denied as part of everyday life for millions of women.'

I am aware of a certain community where dowry is at least fifty to sixty thousand dollars, sometimes even more. I have to question where a young man who has just commenced working is expected to come up with this ridiculous offer—and some families expect a wedding on top of that? From my own point of view, because we are human it then becomes natural for men in these cultures to expect great services from these women and when this is not done, frustration turns into anger. In my opinion, wouldn't it be better to help the young ones settle comfortably rather than stressing on working for dowry or even getting loans? In Australia, fifty to sixty thousand dollars is a deposit for a house.

From the conversations that I have had with many young women in contemporary times, the thought of dowry is daunting and depressing. Personally, I actually had depression and nightmares just thinking about it because I didn't know how much my husband would be charged for dowry. Everyone I know who has gone through the process of dowry before me has never said anything positive; before the marriage has begun, already harsh words have been passed around and relationships tested through the negotiations. It takes a strong and forgiving couple to continue in their marriage happily after that.

To other people, the customary law of dowry is okay and comfortable, but to me it was the most uncomfortable conversation I have had. I love my African tradition and culture, however, there are some things I personally feel need revaluation. After seeing women abused and being cheated on in the name of 'I paid dowry', I made a personal decision that when it came to my time to get married, whatever the cost, I would pay half of the dowry. I was never going to allow another man to put a finger on me because he made some sort of payment for me to become his. I was never going to allow a man to put higher expectations on me because of the dollar value he had paid. Even though this

Chapter Two: Introduction to Domestic Violence and Abuse

is not spoken about, I believe it is a conversation that needs to be heard and started in communities and families who practise this customary law.

I grew up hearing abused women say that they were staying only for the sake of their children, bless their hearts. Practically, it sounds right, as two parents provide a good and safe environment for their children and if the husband is a breadwinner it becomes even more complicated. For how long does one have to put up with abuse? To the mothers who are staying in abusive relationships for the sake of their children, all I can advise is don't be ashamed to share your toxic marriage struggles, because you are not the only one struggling. According to the president of the women's advisory council, Liz Byrski, 'children are better off in a one-person, non-violent family situation than a two-parent, violent family situation. Children can actually be relieved to be removed from a violent situation. There are many one parent families that are successfully bringing up their children and teaching them that it is not alright to use violence in the home.' In the wake of the Harvey Weinstein scandal, how many actresses have spoken out? Previously, some were ashamed to speak out because they thought they were the only ones, but how many people have come out now?

To the women out there: stop giving yourself excuses for speaking out (such as for the sake of kids, family, career or religion you practise, etc.). Do you ever question that you might be giving your kids a bad example of the concept of marriage or family? When he or she grows up they may repeat the same process. Do you ever ask your kids if they really want to stay in these environments, since you are doing it for them?

A few people have argued with me that the Bible talks against divorce, but I am yet to read a scripture that says it is okay to use your wife as a punching bag. To the young women: just because our role models (whether a mother, grandmother, aunty, guardian, etc.) are strong enough to stay in an unhealthy relationship does not mean that we are obligated to stay in unhealthy relationships. Sad as it is to say, every relationship is different. What works for one might not work for another. To the young women: we are not our elders, they have their own reasons for trying to save their marriages, but that is not our obligation. Even though I ended up in a situation I didn't want to be in, the determination to be in a good relationship is what kept me going during that difficult time of abuse, because deep down I knew I did not deserve to be abused. And here I am today, happily married to a gentleman who respects me—to the extent of opening the car door for me—something I still cannot get over after my previous experience of abuse and disrespect. I remember in our days of courting, my now husband and I could meet up for a movie and afterwards he would follow me home and make sure I had parked my car in the garage and then he would eventually drive off to his place. I saw a man who was truly interested in my safety before anything else.

In the years of being abused, I am confident to say that I was not perfect, but I was a good person and I knew it. I did not deserve the ill treatment I received. In my culture there is a saying: *mukadzi mutsvuku akasaba anoroya*, meaning 'a light-skinned woman is either a thief or witch'. I was so quiet and calm—even though I was being abused—and I would just look and listen, which made him more furious, and he would say, 'no wonder they say "Mukadzi mutsvuku akasaba anoroya", you should be a witch.' When I think of these words I realise that he knew what he was doing. He was poking and poking to get a reaction, which I did not give him. I used to laugh deep inside because it was funny, I thought it was ridiculous—a witch, of all things. He probably knew how strong I was mentally and the only way to kill my spirit was to equate me to a witch. If you are a strong woman, does it mean you are a witch? This is another example of African culture which calls for deconstruction; some of the traditional sayings, such as the one I have just mentioned about light-skinned women, reinforce cultural baggage which is illogical and disempowering.

In the times we are living in, domestic violence is talked about day in and day out. The governments are trying all they can to bring awareness and stop violence in families. Ignorance is not an excuse, however, *fear* is a big hindrance to our freedom. I can only say that you are the only person who can free yourself from the toxic relationship and you have to fight that spirit of fear. A scripture which I constantly remind myself of is in 2 Timothy 1:7, which states, 'For God has not given us a spirit of fear, but of power and of love and of a sound mind.' I repeat: FIGHT THE SPIRIT OF FEAR!!!

Chapter Two: Introduction to Domestic Violence and Abuse

Saul constantly reminded me that if it was not for him, I would not be in Australia—he constantly threatened to cancel the spouse visa. For example, if we disagreed on anything Saul would remind me that I had struggled to pay my fees and he had helped me with my visa issues, so had it not been for him, I would not be in Australia. He was right in a way, and I was just scared of him reporting me to immigration, as I thought that would be the end of my legal residence in Australia. However, I am here to say that if you do your homework well, the government system will help you because they know people like this exist. You are not the first and neither are you the last. It is not easy but you can do it, as I did.

There is absolutely nothing wrong with practising spirituality or being religious, but when it is used to disadvantage others then we all have a right to question the motives and intentions behind it. Having been part of different youth groups, I have come to realise that most of the young girls are as naïve as I was. Our elders do not encourage dating at all and only talk about marriage. For one to marry, shouldn't they know the other person and be allowed to see if they are compatible first? Isn't a good marriage built on a strong foundation through the dating experience? I see so many young people talking about marriage and babies, yet they don't even have the tools for good communication or understand what a good relationship is. For my part, regardless of how many times he asked me for my hand in marriage, I was not getting married to him until he changed, so babies were not even in the picture. I responded to my situation by praying and fasting for my boyfriend to change—alas, nothing changed. Now I realise there is more to God, the Holy Spirit, prayer, fasting, faith, believing, speaking in tongues and all. Relationships need to be worked on by *both* individuals. I focused more on the spiritual possibilities, whilst the physical, financial and emotional side of the relationship went downhill. As an afterthought, though, maybe it did work, and that's why I am still alive today.

Lately, I am outraged by how naïve the youth are in their desire to have celebrity-like relationships. Beautifully photoshopped pictures of smart looking spiritual leaders with their spouses are shared across Facebook and Instagram, and people are told 'if you want a relationship like ours, type *amen* and receive what we have, or buy anointing oil and your relationship will be on fire.' As a society, we need to be asking the question: are we preparing the young generation about the reality of relationships and marriage? If our young ones knew how these people treat each other privately, would they believe what they say? Who is responsible for this? Charity begins at home and I believe this conversation should start with the parents and guardians. There is a scripture in Hosea 4:6 that says 'My people are destroyed from lack of knowledge.' A word of advice: do not be too spiritual in the natural, as a quote from Alfred Alder says, 'Follow your heart but take your brain with you.'

Christianity does not condone abuse, yet it happens and is not discussed. As a young and innocent woman, I thought I could change my boyfriend because I was innocent, fresh and worth it. Ha! Life has no such formulas. We cannot change anyone but ourselves.

Chapter Three

MY HEART

There are two ways to live your life. One is as though nothing is a miracle. The other is as though everything is a miracle

— Albert Einstein

CHAPTER THREE

MY HEART

Having been given a second chance, I take life seriously; I don't use the word death lightly when speaking, because I know my purpose, which is to serve others. But it is also important to my other half, my husband, to whom I made the vow, 'to love and to cherish, from this day forward until death do us part'. My life is also very important to my family, friends and, above all, God, who has the authority to take it anytime and any day without anyone's permission.

Today, the 5th of September 2017, as I sit determined to finish this book, I have mixed emotions. I have felt like giving up on this book, if not giving up on my life, as I have gone through dark times. This book is based on my life, and because I have lived my life with other people, unfortunately my

Chapter Three: My Heart

recitation of events and view of the world has not been comparable to others around me. This makes the task of recollection difficult at times. I recall that for the past six weeks I have had to endure sleepless nights and nightmares because of the emotional stress of being misinterpreted by my loved ones for my reasons behind writing this book.

I have had moments when I wished God could open up my heart and show my loved ones what is deep down in my heart, but unfortunately, this is not possible. Twice—if not, thrice—in the past weeks, I have secretly asked God to take me to Him in my sleep because the burden was too much to carry. I have been telling God that I have written the things He put in my heart and I have paid the publisher, so He can just take me and then the book will be published when I am gone, but that would show cowardice. If I was doing this for myself or for fame it would be another story, but my passion and love for seeing abused people get strong and go on to live beautiful lives is so strong—I cannot give up. To see the young people going through relationship struggles, overcome them and see the light at the end of the tunnel, brings so much joy to my heart, and unfortunately it has cost me much.

I often ask myself if writing this book is worth it. The answer is a big *YES*. Friday the 31st of March 2017, I was involved in a car accident, and after I had come out of the shock, the first thing that came to my mind was regret. I prayed a simple prayer, 'Thank you God for saving me in this accident because I would have regretted not telling all the abused people of my story and encourage them that there is life, joy, peace and love in abundance after abuse if they seek help.' Even though I had started writing the book a few months before, I was not done yet and I felt like this was a close call, and soon afterwards I recorded a few videos on domestic violence. To me, if I was going to die soon, at least those videos on YouTube and Facebook, and all the people I have shared with my story on abuse, would be something. And if God asked me what I had done with the life He spared me a couple of times, I thought to myself that I would at least say I encouraged a few people and did not just keep my testimony to myself. As Pastor John Hagge said, 'Your story is the key that can unlock someone else's prison. Share your testimony.'

When I remember how I felt then, how scared I was of dying when I thought I still had an assignment to finish, I ask myself why I now think it's worth it to die because of a few discouragements, judgements, rejections, misunderstandings and anger towards my life story. When I was being abused I had the same feeling I am feeling now: that no one could understand what I was going through. Having come out of it, I now understand that there are so many people going through abuse in different cultures, nations and continents. It is unfortunate that society encourages people to be silent. Just because I had not opened up my mouth to confide in someone going through the same situation as me doesn't mean I was the only one suffering; hundreds if not millions of people are being abused and some dying in the process. I know this feeling too well, being misunderstood, judged and blamed. The sadness, grief, loneliness and sorrow can push me to do the unthinkable, however, the little voices of encouragement I have received is what is keeping me going. So, to all the people who have encouraged and helped me on this journey: thank you so much.

Chapter Three: My Heart

MOVING TO A FOREIGN LAND

Wherever you go, go with your heart

— Confucius

I left Zimbabwe on the 18th of July in 2004, soon after graduating from high school. As mentioned earlier, I could not even point to Australia on a map. My parents researched and chose Perth as my next destination for continuing my studies, bless their hearts, and I will forever be grateful for the opportunity they gave me. They made the decision, against all odds, to ensure that I completed my higher education in Australia. The process and resources required for an international student to travel overseas are not for the faint hearted. I felt like giving up at times, as it was a long process and you needed to pass all requirements so I could not imagine what my parents were going through during that time.

So even though I sympathised with their sacrifices for bringing me to Australia, personally I did not have the most affectionate relationship with my family then. Though I was surprised at Harare International airport when I gave my dad a hug and burst into tears, I couldn't even explain what happened. The love was there but I just did not have the best way of communicating with them and I felt like I was constantly in a hide and seek game.

And I got even more annoyed with my family because life was so difficult settling down in Perth and at times I wished I had just stayed at home, but looking back now I realise that God had other plans: for me to be in Australia. I had to learn over time to forgive them because they didn't know where I was going either and they are such a blessing in my life. I wouldn't change anything. Our relationship has grown and changed over the years; I am now more open and I talk a lot. I reflect on the number of people who are deported or returned to their native countries unwillingly because of various reasons. Here, I am now settled and happy in Australia—everything happened for a reason.

I came to Australia with a few friends, and they were all I had. It is funny that we grew up together and even went to high school for six years together, but unfortunately, we were not close. However, being in a foreign land where everything was different to how we grew up, we soon learnt that it was only us and no one else. I remember late night walks up and down South Street in Fremantle, and it was just so beautiful passing by cafes and pubs. This is something we could never do in Zimbabwe, as it was assumed that we were meeting guys. As a girl child, you could not even ask to go for a walk at night, only in your dreams. The new freedom away from parents was a bit too much for us, the students. With more new friends we ventured into clubbing, tried alcohol—oh yes, we loved Baileys—and other experiments that other young people were into.

Initially, I had arranged to stay with Nothando, a friend's daughter whom I knew. The plan was that I would stay with her until I familiarised myself with Perth, got myself a job, and then I would eventually get a place to rent. Life is not always that rosy, though, and for some unknown reason, Nothando did not come back to Australia from her holidays. I still went to her place and lived with her housemate, who did not look pleased by my presence. After two weeks, the housemate asked me to find a place to stay as she was planning on leaving and finding cheaper accommodation since her roommate was not returning to Australia.

I did not even know where to start; I was just getting to know my surroundings and I had to leave. The next day, I went to school and asked the student services if they could help me find cheap accommodation closer to school. I was told to look on the notice board to see if anyone was looking for a housemate and I could not find anything. I gave the student services my email so they

Chapter Three: My Heart

could forward me any accommodation and casual job offers for students. The very following morning I had two emails with positive feedback. A lady was looking for a stay-in student and another lady who happened to be studying at Notre Dame University was looking for a cleaner. This was just too good to be true and I called the ladies, we met up and, as they say, the rest was history.

Without wasting any more time, I moved out the following day to Fremantle as this place was just ten minutes from the university. I would instantly save on transport as I went on the free bus. So, for the next six months in Perth I lived with a beautiful lady by the name of Cathy. Cathy had a newborn baby and needed a stay-in student who could assist with babysitting duties whilst she was at work. Looking back, God used her as a vessel to teach me love in a foreign land where there was absolutely no one older to take care of me. I love my family dearly and I know they love me, I just needed to come to realise it on my own, as I had a lot of misunderstandings within myself. After coming to Australia, I saw a different way of showing love. From my own perspective, white people are more affectionate than most Africans and more open with their feelings. Personally, I find most African men do not smile, as they try to put on this strong persona, but is it really worth it? Cathy could openly tell me how she appreciated what I did; she hugged me or kissed me and showed me love in a way that was mind-blowing and that I had never experienced. I felt more than at home. There is a purpose and a reason why we meet different people in our lives. At times, it doesn't make sense, but eventually it all comes together when you take time to reflect and look back.

I had to pay Cathy $50 a week for accommodation, meals included, and honestly, all meals were delicious. Even though all the food was different and new, I do not ever remember disliking anything. I still remember the oats she made for breakfast with pear fruit and raisins in them, and the nachos she made with beans. Every weekend we visited her parents down south in Rockingham and they treated me like a *queen*—I could not believe it, but that was all God. I had my own pink bedroom, I was served all meals and did not cook, just stacked dishes in the dishwasher. Cathy's brother lived next door to the parents, and when they realised I loved cleaning I would go and clean for at least three hours and get a little reward.

As mentioned earlier, the week I found accommodation with Cathy I also found a cleaning job and I was only getting $50 for three hours per week. Talk about God meeting you on your point of needs; it is just what I required. After a few weeks, I found another cleaning job at a nearby bakery close to the house, and this was now like pocket money; I could buy a few things I needed and bus fare to move me from one place to another. Life was just perfect—I am happy to admit that I never felt homesick. I was truly enjoying my independence and new environment, there was so much to see and learn.

In December 2004, my landlady Cathy wanted to travel, so she asked me if a few of my friends could move in with me. Unfortunately, they all did not want to stay at the house so me and my friends decided it was time to explore Australia and be independent without a mother figure. I moved in with my friends into an unfurnished apartment and we bought every single thing in this house together, from the spoons to everything else. If you know your purpose, Australia can be the land of milk and honey, as people say. Who would have thought that young girls who have just been in Perth for six months from Zimbabwe, with nothing, could furnish an apartment?

Before I knew it, the world was in my hands: working, studying, clubbing and just enjoying life. Independence can be so great when you are young and free, but too much freedom can also spoil you if you are not careful. Ecclesiastes 11:9 says, 'Young people, enjoy your youth. Be happy while you are still young. Do what you want to do, and follow your heart's desire. But remember that God is going to judge you for whatever you do.'

Chapter Three: My Heart

MEETING SAUL—25TH DECEMBER 2004

One day, you will meet someone and then you know that your search is over ... because you've found your special someone

— Dooset Daram Plazche

So, who is Saul Wena? I met the handsome, tall, funny and outspoken guy on Christmas Day in 2004. We were attending a Christmas lunch at one of the church elders' houses and so we had to pass by Saul's house to pick him up, as he did not know the way. He had a brand-new Toyota Camry, so I decided to drive with him to the elder's house because his car was more beautiful than the one I was in before. As I write, I am cringing, *like really?* A beautiful car caught my eye—there are so many things that can catch your eye that are not for you. A good man is not the car he drives, the shoes he wears, the clothes he has on, the perfume he wears, the house he owns, how much money he has, what job he has, the hairstyle, or swag, as we call it nowadays—'material stuff'.

As a young woman of this generation, I encourage us to move away from the looks, hairstyles, shoe type, cars, houses, money, friends, professions, bling-bling and swag that we see in men. Especially social media, Facebook, Twitter, Instagram, YouTube and Snap Chat—name it all—which have been killers, because at times what we see is not even a tenth of the truth. For the sake of *likes* and popularity, people have thrown their morals into the bin, for example, someone standing next to a BMW does not make them the owner, neither does taking a picture in a hotel room make it their own bedroom. But we are so quick to think the picture is true; well I am here to remind people that we are in the editing and photoshopping era. Anyone can change their outside appearance, but what we need to focus more on is the inside of a person and personality, as mentioned in 1 Samuel 16:7, 'But the Lord said to him, "Pay no attention to how tall and handsome he is. I have rejected him, because I do not judge as people judge. They look at the outward appearance, but I look at the heart.'"

From his outward appearance, people knew Saul as an outgoing person, a church goer, always making people laugh—loved his drink, loved to party, loved soccer—'a massive football fan'—loved children and nice things. However, behind closed doors I saw a bully, a liar who manipulated his way out, who knew what he was doing (which you will read through the book), a two-faced assaulter. No matter what I said to people in regards to what was going on inside the house, he constantly said I was a *drama queen* seeking attention.

I grew up in a non-alcoholic and religious environment, so I was neither taught nor had any experience of alcoholics for nineteen years of my childhood. Nothing could have prepared me for a boyfriend like Saul, so everything was a first. Even the change of behaviour in Saul when he was drunk was a total surprise and shock to me. During our early days of courting, I would visit and find him dead drunk on the couch, or he would visit me at late hours, midnight or 2 am, dead drunk, either driving or by taxi. Being naïve and not knowing what to do, I would just open the door for him and he would crash at our house and then wake up in the morning.

Saul identified himself as a Christian, however, his character was nothing compared to the faith he claimed to believe in. This might not suit some believers, but I personally find nothing wrong with a Christian falling in love with a non-Christian or a person who is different from your beliefs. One of my favourite quotes from Maya Angelou, says, 'Love recognises no barriers. It jumps hurdles, leaps fence, penetrates walls to arrive at its destination full of hope.' The church houses everyone despite their background.

Being a church goer does not qualify a person to be a Christian. Are we not tired and disgusted of hearing in the media about the abuse that occurred in Catholic and Anglican Christian schools? When I look at Saul, who was a Christian, and then compare the qualities of a good man that my now husband (non-Christian) depicts, I would love to encourage others to be open minded and without prejudice.

Chapter Three: My Heart

THE FIRST SIGN OF ABUSE.

Verbal abuse is still abuse. It's abuse in the form of words. Don't assume that a few hurtful words won't cost them their life. Words hurt

—Unknown

As a young girl in love, I thought to myself, as drunk as Saul would be, if he could still remember me and where I lived in that state, then he really loved me. So, it is not surprising that, because of drunken driving, in 2005 Saul was involved in a car accident and he was in hospital for a few days and his car was a write-off. During that time, I was busy with assignments at university. I remember receiving a phone call from Saul in the library informing me of the accident. After learning of the seriousness of the accident I said exasperatedly, 'You are lucky to be alive, how could you drive when you were drunk? You need to change your behaviour before you actually get killed.'

So, when I went to visit Saul in hospital he told me off for disciplining him in front of his friends earlier on the phone. He said I should have first asked him how badly he was injured and the pain he was going through. According to him, I should have shown remorse, as he was in pain, instead of telling him off like he was a child. He said not only was he in pain, but he had just lost his brand-new car, as he had no insurance and he couldn't work for a while, so he would not be able to pay rent. Whilst he was talking, I realised that he wasn't mad at me for telling him off, but rather he was worried about his own upkeep moving on from the accident.

He asked me if I could help him pay for his rent and bills and he would repay me when he started working. Being the kind person I am, I paid for all his bills and I remember Liz Panyamanhete, one of my housemates, was annoyed with me for doing this. I did not have enough money for myself, but there I was paying for his bills. And I can report back that I never got a cent back from all the bills I paid.

Saul and I always argued, as we were never on the same page. I was upset with him one day and whilst chatting on the phone I asked him if we could break up, and he refused. I cannot recall why I was upset on this particular occasion, and because I asked to end the relationship he called his Papa (his adopted father) to talk to me on his behalf. I remember getting a call from Papa whilst I walked on South Street in Fremantle and he was talking about relationships and how Saul was very sorry for his behaviour and if I could please forgive him. I vividly recall telling Papa that he did not understand and he was arguing with me that he was older and knew a bit about relationships through experience. I repeatedly argued that he did not understand, as this was always my mentality that African elders never understood the younger people. I thought I always had to defend myself.

Eventually, I met Papa, who later introduced me to his wife, Mama, and their children. Before I knew it, I was head over heels in love with this family and this outraged Saul, as I began to spend more time with them. Saul's jealousy grew to rage. He would persistently accuse me of spending more time with his family than himself and he would remind me that had it not been for him I wouldn't have known them. That all fell on deaf ears because I couldn't get enough of them, as I had found a place of belonging. I call it a divine connection because we met and we just clicked and I became a part of the family. For some unknown reason, Mama started calling me her asset/profit and Saul would see red.

A few weeks later, on one of my visits to Saul's house after cleaning because he was too drunk to give me the attention, I bid him farewell. He was not happy because he wanted me to stay overnight—after all, he was a recovering patient. I was not ready for sleepovers, and I told him it was time to leave, so I got ready and left. And, yes, I was a virgin then, waiting for marriage before sex.

He followed me from his house to the train station and was very agitated because he kept asking me why I did not want to stay over and saying how I never stayed long enough with him. I told him, 'I am always around. It is just that you are too drunk to even have a normal conversation'. As we crossed the

Chapter Three: My Heart

road from his unit to the other side of the road in broad daylight, at around five in the evening, we kept arguing and I turned to face him and he just slapped me right across the face; *ouch*, that really hurt. Before he could give me another one I held my hands over my face and could feel the tingling on my face. Those who look at me now and think I am small should have seen me back then—I was way too skinny and tiny and I just saw black. When I opened my eyes, I still felt like something had been thrown on my face and I was opening my mouth and feeling my face to check all was good. Then the floodgates of tears just opened and they flowed down my face.

At first, I was shocked that with so many cars and public strangers around I had just been slapped right across the face with his big hands. Then came the anger—how dare he try to force me to stay at his house—and then the pain from my face. My mind went into an overdrive of mixed emotions. I could not even remember when I had last been belted, because I was never, ever smacked on the face. I just walked quickly to the train in full blown tears, and no matter how much he tried to apologise and sympathise I was not having any of it. How could I be smacked for wanting to go back to my own house? Why could we not just be in love without the pressure of having sex? The thought of Loverboy, who I had left in Zimbabwe, came back; for four years he never forced me, nor did we ever talk of sex because it was out of question. That was the day I should have run for the hills and never looked back. I was naïve; I didn't.

The guilt of what he had just done made him follow me home. In the train from Glendalough to Perth City I was in tears; no matter how much I tried to understand what had just happened, nothing made sense. The security guards came close to our seat and I just looked down, as we looked very suspicious, and he tried hard to console me. I changed trains from Perth City to Fremantle and then a bus from Fremantle to Hamilton Hill and he still followed me till I got home. I went straight to bed and did not tell my housemates what had happened because he was right there, and he slept over out of fear of what I was going to do or say. He kept apologising the whole night that he was a bit drunk, as most people do. Alcohol should never be an excuse for anyone to abuse another person. And yes, I believed him—well he had spent the whole night apologising, caressing the face he had slapped and crying. I felt remorse, after all, he promised me he would never ever do it again, I believed him and that in itself was another mistake.

I don't know if it was paranoia, jealousy or that the controlling man in him was coming out, but whenever he called me he expected me to answer the phone. He could have been a telemarketer—he always rang me non-stop. If I was at work, university, or my phone was on silent, how could I answer it? I remember very well my ringtone was *Hips Don't Lie* by Shakira. My workmates used to ask me how I coped with the phone ringing all the time because even in their sleep at night my ringtone played out in their heads. Imagine, if others were affected, how it was for me when I had the phone on me 24/7.

I had to ask, did he not believe I was at work, did he not believe that I was out with my friends or in the library studying? Anytime and anyplace he could just pop up literally, so his phone was his controlling device. I remember one night we went clubbing with my girlfriends—it was our girls' night out—and then from nowhere I saw him right behind me because I had told him where we were going. All the girls just rolled their eyes. I cannot count how many jobs he lost because he was never at the worksite; instead, he was busy coming home, probably to check if I was there and not with anyone else.

This became my routine and new life; that slapping on Harborne Street became what he called a practical joke for the rest of our relationship. He would occasionally, after an argument or misunderstanding, taunt me over the phone that he was coming over to hit the crap out of me. I remember the first day he joked like that I felt the chill in my bones. I came home from a cleaning job and literally took a duvet blanket and sat in the sitting room with the heater on and just waited anxiously with my phone in my hand for him to turn up at the front door. I remember calling an acquaintance (Vince) that was aware of the violent relationship I was in and telling him that Saul had just threatened to come and hit me and Vince asked me if he should call the police, and I said no. Believe it or not, I actually got burnt on my arm with the heater—I woke up with blisters and the duvet was burnt as well. How can

Chapter Three: My Heart

one use such a practical joke to taunt another person? He would occasionally call telling me how near he was and I was always a nervous wreck—that is how much I had become scared of him, without even realising it. At times, I could look through the window waiting anxiously to see him, but he was just lying, he would be miles away from me. Abuse is not just physical, it can be emotional and psychological, as you can see. He was not around me all the time, but even when he was not, I still felt his abusive presence.

Chapter Four

LOSING MY VIRGINITY

Life is too short, time is too precious, and the stakes are too high to dwell on what might have been

— Hillary Clinton

CHAPTER FOUR

LOSING MY VIRGINITY

It was a big deal to me, losing my virginity, because of my upbringing and being a Christian. I had envisioned losing my womanhood to my husband on our first night together and having the best time of our lives, as I saw in movies and all. Real life, at times, is different from our dreams and fantasies. After a few arguments and quarrels about us being intimate, I eventually gave in one night because I thought to myself, he is going to be my husband after all, as long as I stay with him God will understand. Saul knew what a big deal this was to me and I thought we were on the same page and that he would respect me.

That first night together turned out to be my worst nightmare. I cannot remember the nitty gritties of the process. As soon as I realised what had happened, I got emotional and started crying. I then realised that I was no longer a virgin and if things did not work out, I was doomed for life, as the next guy would not respect me knowing I was not a virgin. That is when I remembered all the talk about getting tested before sex, *hahaha, I have to chuckle here*. Funnily enough, I did not think of protection or getting pregnant. I cannot recount how many times I was advised to abstain from sex. *Hello*, who would have thought that after sex you start thinking so much? That is why I should have stuck to my guns, especially if I knew I would think like this, right?

Saul got annoyed with me for crying for some reason. He had this look that he used to give me when he was agitated and I would just know that things were about to turn upside down. I do not know how he was feeling, but I can guess that he was proud to have worked hard for months to get to this stage. He asked me why I was crying and when I did not respond he started yelling at me and said that I was making him to look like a monster who had

Chapter Four: Losing My Virginity

raped me and so he got up, dressed and walked out. My worst nightmare was becoming the reality that 'men eat the cake' and disappear. This made me annoyed and I was outraged. I felt like a thief had stolen a precious jewel of mine. He returned later and tried to comfort me and all, but the damage had been done.

In accordance with African culture, I grew up knowing that after my wedding night the elders and aunties would ask for the white sheet my husband and I had slept on, to inspect it for blood. If there was none, they would not respect me at all. This is another reason why it took me so long to leave Saul, because I thought I was doomed for life; this shows you how immature and naïve I was. I am not the first and will not be the last to think this way. As I reflect, these beliefs about virginity and marriage were also consequences of cultural socialisation and religious indoctrination. I am now happily married and my husband adores me, so there is no truth to what I grew up hearing. Although this does not offer permission to sleep around, as there are some cultures that still practice checking one's virginity. Maybe there is a little truth—there are still some traditional families—but if you and your husband know the truth, should there be a big problem? I understand that the elders want to scare the young ones from sleeping around, but why do they never tell us the other side of the story? Aren't the expectations of virginity at the time of marriage contradicted by the pressures from boys to prove their coming of age by sleeping with the girls?

I will not be giving advice about sex before marriage, because it is all about individual choices—I heard all the advice in the world, but look at what I went through. We could argue for days, years or even centuries. Let each person do what is right and let God be the judge. Listen to that voice inside of you and obey it. It would not have been a surprise had I missed my period. After a few weeks of contemplating this, as I was scared and didn't know who to open up to, I finally got the courage to talk to Kiri (a nurse friend), who advised me to go to the hospital and be checked. Yes, I had fallen pregnant, but I had miscarried. I had to stay overnight so they could get rid of the residue, whatever that meant.

Reflecting on whether I knew about contraception, it was never a point of discussion growing up because I was expected to have sex only after I was married. In my circles, I never heard a conversation on contraception. Only in school, during social studies, was it encouraged to use condoms. Saul and I had used condoms, however, one time the condom got stuck inside me. The panic and wrestle it took to have it taken out of me made me scared and I decided not to use condoms, as it would be embarrassing if it happened again and I would need to go to the hospital—I was extremely shy then. I started taking the pill, but because I was ignorant and always forgot to take them consistently, I found myself in the same situation: pregnant.

Throughout our relationship, for some unknown reason, Saul used to torment me, and occasionally joke that I was not a virgin when he met me. I used to see red as he was the only man I knew sexually—why would he dare say such a thing? I don't know if it was a psychological game he played to make me angry, but this would make me blow out. We could actually get into a serious argument, that is how far his practical jokes would go. He would then tease me, telling me that he was just playing practical jokes on me because he knew how angry I got. *Ummmm, really?* Does one have to go this far, to watch the person they truly love cry and get upset? Saul was a bully and intentionally teased me; he inflicted fear and anxiety on me.

It was now coming towards the end of 2005, and after almost a year of pure bliss living with my housemates, they took their independence to the next level, and I could not tolerate it anymore. Personally, I believe anyone is free to date whosoever they like, but I do not appreciate any person who gets in relations with a married person knowingly because I grew up seeing many families destroyed with this selfish behaviour. So, when one of my housemates did this selfish act of being involved with a married man, I lost it. Then to add insult to injury, Saul told me off like there was no tomorrow because of their behaviour. I remember our phone conversation: 'Tinashe, how can I even trust you when you live with people like that. If they can behave like this, how can I be assured that when I am not around you are not

Chapter Four: Losing My Virginity

behaving the same? You girls are pretending to be little innocent angels yet in fact you are not.' I was not only shocked, I was outraged, because at this point in time I did not even know what he was talking about. So, I asked him what the problem was and he asked me to check my housemates. I was working night shifts so I did not know what happened during my absence.

Knowing him, the first thought was that Saul was just trying to come between me and my friends so I would move out and stay with him. I was timid then; I still struggled with my communication skills, but I was curious to know what was going on because I had really coughed up on their behalf. Ultimately, one night I just burst in and confronted them and came to realise that we had all grown to have different approaches to life and that led to the breakdown of our relationships. I told them I was moving out the following day, which I happily did, and since then we have lived independently, as far away as possible from each other.

I then asked Saul if I could move in with him for a while whilst I sorted myself out; I just packed my clothes and left. On his part he was delighted, as he had been asking for this forever—was I reckless? I do not know. In African culture it is taboo for an unmarried girl to move in with her boyfriend without him paying dowry to the girls' parents. By paying dowry the guy gets consent to live (and obviously be sexually active) with the girl. I had mixed emotions, as I felt that I was doing the wrong thing by my culture, but because I was already intimate with Saul, I felt it was unnecessary to feel guilty. Not to mention, in my new environment there was nothing wrong with a girl of my age living with her partner in a de-facto relationship.

According to the family Court of Australia, a de facto relationship is defined in Section 4AA of the Family Law Act 1975. 'The law requires that you and your former partner, who may be of the same or opposite sex, had a relationship as a couple living together on a genuine domestic basis. However, your relationship is not a de facto relationship if you were legally married to one another or if you are related by family.' I thought I knew what I was asking for—to live with him—as he was going to be working up North of Western Australia, so I had planned to take care of his house whilst I sorted myself out.

At times, not only does it rain, it pours. To make matters worse, when my results for that semester came out, unfortunately I failed my core accounting unit. The school sent my letters to the old address where I was staying with my housemates, asking that I visit the dean of the college regarding counselling. For some reason, the letter never reached me, but was instead sent to Zimbabwe, addressed to my parents. Reflecting back, it was my responsibility as a student to change my details with the university and follow up on my results. However, because I was distracted, with so many things going on, I was not responsible enough. But that did not give anyone the right to forward personal information on to my parents; I assume it was payback on my housemates' behalf, that out of spite they sent the letter to Zimbabwe (I could be wrong, but I will never know).

It took a while for the letter to reach Zimbabwe (as you can imagine) and when my parents received it, they rang me to advise me to call the school. I went to meet the dean of college only to be told I had been negligent and that they had tried to contact me to no avail, therefore I needed to visit the immigration department. When you are an international student and you are told to visit the immigration department, no matter how healthy you think you are, that very moment you feel every symptom of fever—I felt sick.

I was in shock from what I heard from the faculty dean and so I dashed to the immigration office, only to be told my student visa had been cancelled. They advised me that I was not taking my studies seriously and I was given twenty-eight days to leave Australia. To be honest, until today I cannot understand or explain what happened with my student visa cancellation. Those who have been or are international students will understand how families sacrifice everything, and the fees are not to be joked about. For this to happen was like a bullet shot right through my heart.

Chapter Four: Losing My Virginity

I was mad, furious, upset and confused; I felt everything you can think of. My first thought was *how could I go back to Zimbabwe without finishing my studies and face my family who had sacrificed everything?* I could not think of how I could start a conversation about failing and not taking my studies seriously. So, I vowed to never see nor speak to my housemates. I phoned and confronted them about their actions and they denied any involvement, which irritated me even more. Whether they did forward the letter to my parents or not I will never know, that was it between us I thought—out of sight, out of mind!

CHANGE FROM INTERNATIONAL STUDENT VISA TO SPOUSE VISA

Every cloud has a silver lining

—D.R. Locke (1863)

Going back to the immigration saga, I had been given twenty-eight days to leave the country. According to the Department of Immigration and Citizenship (DIAC), a visa applicant is usually given a 28-day period to respond to the refusal to grant a visa. This gives you, the applicant, the opportunity to show DIAC why your visa should not be denied or reverse the immigration decision. Saul suggested that he was happy to try and apply for the spouse visa, as we had been in a relationship for more than a year, as per the requirements. It was worth a try—after all, I had nothing to lose. We discussed our decision and we thought this would be a great idea, so the following day we were back at the immigration department and, of course, they thought I was just applying for the spouse visa because I was desperate.

However, the officer told me to try and apply for the spouse visa but this was not guaranteed. The requirements were to prove that we had been staying together in the same dwelling for a year and that all of my mail was being delivered to this place. We needed photographic evidence showing we had been in a relationship for the whole year of 2005. Had events begun to prove more difficult, I could have just packed my bags that very day and left for Zimbabwe. I had nothing to show for myself but I scrounged for whatever I could find and submitted an application. After that, all I could do was hope and pray for the best. We were called in for an interview and it was nerve-racking; my life was in God's hands, literally. I was told to just wait for the results, and within a few days I found out that I had been successful and got the spouse visa. The condition was that we stay together in the relationship for two whole years and then I would qualify for a permanent residency. I had always heard of miracles, and this would turn out to be the first miracle of my life.

I was free to work, continue with my studies and do anything I wanted. What a miracle and a blessing this was. I was grateful to Saul for giving me this chance in life; you would think I had the world at my feet now, but this spouse visa became my hell. From that very moment, till the day I left this relationship, for every decision or plan I made, I was accused of being arrogant because I was on a spouse visa. In every relationship, people are bound to disagree, but I could not say no to something without being reminded that he had helped me to stay in Australia on his visa. This became his weakness and downfall, as well as a prison for me.

SECOND PREGNANCY

At the bottom of patience one finds heaven

—African proverb

From childhood, I had never enjoyed taking medication when ill; this became a weakness in trying to use contraception—I was just hopeless. I took the contraceptive pill for a while, but I missed so many days in between that I eventually gave up. As a result, I ended up pregnant again (after the miscarriage) and in my crazy mind I tried to do what I thought was the right thing to do and go along with the pregnancy. One day I went to visit Kiri (my nurse friend) and her hubby Mukoma, whom I had met through Saul. Kiri and Mukoma were the first Zimbabwean friends I met here and we all just fell in love with each other. So, on this particular day when I went to visit them, as soon as Kiri saw me she asked if I was pregnant, as my bust had grown bigger. I laughed and denied it. After more than eight weeks of being extremely ill with morning sickness, mixed with confusion and guilt, I decided I was not having the baby.

I told Mama and Papa that I was pregnant but had decided to terminate the pregnancy. They counselled me and advised me not to go ahead with the termination and to think again, but I had made up my mind. I told Saul I was terminating the pregnancy because I did not want to have the baby. Personally, I was not ready mentally or emotionally and I could not take care of myself properly. *How could I be expected to take care of a child?* I knew what I was capable of handling, and a child was definitely not one of them. I could have gone ahead and listened to Saul, Mama and Papa, however, at the end of the day I was to be responsible for this child and I knew deep down my heart I did not want it.

Reflecting on my decision to terminate the pregnancy, this had to be the only way out. As much as people think they know what is best for you at times, individuals are more capable of knowing what is best for themselves and should not be judged for their decisions. Many times, I have seen and heard of women who have dumped newborn babies or killed them because they listened to other people. They went ahead and did what they thought to be the right thing with the pregnancies and ended up doing the unthinkable, and everyone asks *how can a mother do that to her child?*

In the environment I grew up in, I was surrounded by older women of age who were old enough to be married, let alone have boyfriends. The surprising thing was that even though they were older they were still not expected to be in relationships. It was as if they were only expected to marry but not go through the dating stage. So growing up, I saw many of these women involved in secretive relationships, involved sexually with their boyfriends, and some got pregnant. All of them found medicine and herbs somewhere and terminated their pregnancies by themselves out of fear of being found out. As a result, it felt natural for me to terminate and not be found out. I

Chapter Four: Losing My Virginity

could not think of myself having a child out of wedlock to begin with—what would my family, church and society say? I went to the doctor for a consultation and they told me I was far too far long to get a termination and this would be dangerous.

I plainly told them that it would be the death of me—whichever way, they needed to get this baby out. I talked of my plans with Saul, so this was not a surprise to him: we were in this together. Saul loved kids and he was happy for me to have this baby, but I was not having it and I told him my decision was final. I am very grateful to him for allowing me the opportunity to choose what I thought was right for me because at the end of the day I was the one to carry the pregnancy. The day eventually came to go to the clinic—early morning, from memory, I think it was around four-thirty—and it was dark outside; only bad things happen in darkness, I have to say. And *bang*, to my surprise I met one of my old housemates at the entrance door. Talk about birds of the same feather flocking together. I do not know why she was there, so I will not speculate. Ha! God has the greatest sense of humour in this world. I pretended to be so ill that I could not talk, and just said hello and minded my own business.

The appointment had already been made, so how could I then leave and pretend I was not in an abortion clinic? The time for the procedure came and I went into the surgery room. All I remember seeing were a few nurses in blue uniforms standing around putting on gloves, big lights over the bed and a tray beside me that had surgical instruments. After I was given the anaesthetic I was gone—into another world. I cannot recall the time they expected me to wake up but I went way over the time limit. I was told that the medical team tried to rouse me but I could not wake up. While in my unconscious state, a thought or voice came to me:

When I was very young in Zimbabwe, probably in primary school, a lady in the church had prophesied that she could see me one day falling pregnant and aborting. In the midst of it all I would lose my life. So, she asked very old women in the church to go with me to a secluded place and they prayed for me, and I remember laughing within me, saying how she dare say such embarrassing things to me, how could I get pregnant out of wedlock and abort. This was hilarious then, but right there on the recovery bed (I had a delayed recovery from anaesthesia) something that had happened in my young life came to me. And a voice or thought came to me reminding me that in that instance I was still alive because of the Grace of God. Those old women I laughed at, their prayers saved me this very day. After I woke up, I was still losing consciousness but the nurses were trying to keep me awake—this experience shook me and I cannot forget it.

As a self-proclaimed practical joker, Saul would later torment me for this very decision: I was a killer who had terminated his child. I would get hurt in the heat of the moment when he brought it up, but after a while I would get over it because I made that decision knowing what I was doing and why I was doing it. It's nothing to be proud of, but at that time of my life, I probably would have killed myself if I could not terminate that pregnancy. I remember one time he brought it up in one of our counselling sessions and the pastor rebuked him, telling him he had gone to the clinic with me so why would he try to insult me now?

When I look back, when I began my relationship with Saul it was the first time I had ever heard of practical joking; he constantly bullied and abused me in the name of practical jokes. For example, in this instance, we talked about the termination, we paid for the bill, and he drove me there and picked me up. He was part of the whole process, so when I look back at his selfish behaviour, I realise that it had psychological implications for me, as I felt hopelessness, fear and self-hate.

Chapter Four: Losing My Virginity

VACUUM CLEANER

Bad friends will prevent you from having good friends

—Gabon proverb

Saul had a great Nigerian friend who respected both of us and treated me like his sister because I would cook *sadza* (a traditional Zimbabwean corn food) for him when he visited. He was always welcome for sleepovers whenever they had late nights. One time, when Saul was away at work, the Nigerian friend called me to borrow the vacuum cleaner. As it was no big deal I agreed, and informed Saul as well. As I was all by myself I did not need to use the vacuum cleaner regularly, so when it was returned Saul was away for work.

Saul was furious and speculated I was having an affair with his friend, and questioned the motives of his friend in coming over while he was away to bring back the vacuum cleaner. Because of his rage he flew back to Perth from work that night, just to prove his point, and kicked me out of the house. As you might expect, he had soothed himself with alcohol on the flight back to Perth and when he arrived he was dead drunk.

I remember the argument escalating to an unnecessary magnitude, because we were screaming at each other face-to-face. Saul lifted his hand to smack me on the face and I managed to run out of the house and hide in one of the shrubs outside. I called Mama and Papa, but unfortunately there was no response. I rang Kiri and Mukoma but I could not reach them either. Lastly, I rang Naz, another friend of ours who lived close by and he came and picked me up. Naz tried to calm Saul but he was not having it. I remember that whilst Saul was on the balcony sipping water, Naz was patting my back to calm me down, as I was crying. Then Saul just threw the bottle of water at me. That night, I went to stay with Naz and his family, and believe it or not, whilst I was in bed sleeping, Saul came to apologise and take me home. Do you think I went back? You guessed wrong. I believed him and went back with him late that night. He told me he was not leaving until we left together, and not wanting to cause trouble at a friends' house we made up. The following day he flew back to work.

FRIEND RELEASED FROM JAIL

You should always listen to your intuition, you know yourself best

—Nkandu Beltz

A friend of Saul had been imprisoned for a few years, accused of rape. On a few occasions, we had gone together to visit him in jail. Upon his release (which I was not aware of), Saul told him to come and stay with me. Saul was still away at work and I was on my own in Perth. As you can picture this, on hearing this news I was outraged, so I asked him, 'How can I stay with someone who has been accused of rape?'

I had felt sorry for this guy because he was a young Zimbabwean, but I was not sure if this rape accusation was true or not. This did not sit well with me and I made my concerns known, however, Saul said he was the only friend to this guy and I had to stay with him until he returned from work. My cry was, 'What if he raped me too?' Clearly, Saul did not have my interests and welfare at heart.

This guy came later in the afternoon and knocked on the door, which I unenthusiastically opened. We talked for a bit. As I was staying by myself, I always had cash around the house and I remember I had probably twenty dollars or more on the television cabinet. I went upstairs to do something, and when I came back the guy had left and so had the money. Probably because I was already paranoid, I quickly noticed the money was gone. I immediately rang Saul to voice my concerns, but of course he thought it was an excuse. I waited for the guy to return—which he did later in the evening, smelling a bit of alcohol—and straightaway I confronted him. He denied taking the money, which infuriated me even more; my patience was running out. I told him how disappointed I was and how I did not trust him. At last, he admitted that he had taken the money to buy cigarettes and he had planned to return it after his prison wages were deposited into his account. I remember telling him he should have just asked. Probably because of the confrontation, he was embarrassed and left, and I don't remember ever seeing him again. I felt like I had the right to be upset with Saul for being disrespectful and not caring about my welfare.

Chapter Four: Losing My Virginity

A VISIT TO NORTHERN WESTERN AUSTRALIA AND A THIRD PREGNANCY

I remember very well that after I got my tax return in July of 2006, I visited Saul, in the north of Western Australia, as I had a few dollars to spare. I was excited at the thought of travelling to a new place. This is a very hot and humid place; upon my arrival, I realised I could not stand the heat. As I stepped off the plane, I had a cardigan on, but the heat and even the air I was breathing was very hot.

Without my knowledge, Saul had asked his boss if I could work as a bar attendant. He asked me to take the offer, but as I had never been to such a hot place in my life, I thought *how could I take this offer?* I was not happy, but needless to say I took the offer and worked at the bar that night. That first night as a bar attendant with guys hitting on me, the smell of alcohol and cigarettes made me sick, and so I refused to return the following night.

I reminded him that I was not coming to work but staying for a few days and going back to Perth. We argued that night but I did not continue to make a point. The following day, whilst at the shops, I booked my flight back to Perth, and he never said anything. We shopped around and everything was okay. As soon as we got home from the shops we put away the shopping and we sat on the couch in the sitting room. Out of nowhere, he said, 'Now that you have money, you are trying to show off. Why did you not tell me this morning that you were going to buy a ticket? You can show off this tax return but it will soon finish and you will have nothing to show off.' Even though I was timid, which he knew, when I answered back it used to take him by surprise and he would get more aggressive.

This time was no exception; I reminded him I had a full-time job and had only taken a week off and not resigned from my job. The argument intensified and we screamed at each other. Here we were, staring at each other like mad bulls, trying to get our points across, and the coward did what he does best and smacked me right across the face, and when I covered my face another smack came through, hitting my covered face. I am not sure what it was, but Saul seemed to like smacking my face more than anything else.

As I covered my face, he kept hitting the top of my head and my hands, as I had coiled up like a ball. I managed to break free from him and got up and ran to the toilet so I could lock the door and call the police. I will never forget how I was beaten like a dog that afternoon. I was not quick enough because he held the toilet door with his foot and he followed me in and was hitting my head as I covered my face. I am in tears as I write. I remember this day because that was something significant: how could someone beat a person like that? I remember looking in the mirror and my face was red, and you could see the marks of his fingers on my face.

The fact that I had bought the ticket made me feel better because the following day I was going back home. And on that day, for the first time ever, I realised how much I hated him and wanted to be away from him. Hate is a big word, but that is how I felt. I had not told anyone that I was pregnant and I felt that there was no way I could ever have a child that looked anything like him. I had planned to tell him on this trip that I was pregnant but just the thought of a person that looked like him made me so mad. So as soon as I got back to Perth I organised the termination of this pregnancy. I remember asking Nicky, a friend, for a loan and lied that I had stomach issues. She asked if I was pregnant and I denied it. I did this all by myself and I was happy with my decision, and to this day I have no regrets.

No matter how unhappy I was, I had to stay with this monster just for the spouse visa, otherwise how could I go back to Zimbabwe, and what would I tell my parents? I was also in a dilemma as he had continuously tormented me that I was just with him for the visa, which was true, but I was also trying to prove to him and other people that initially it was love and I was not angry or upset because I now had the right to live in Australia. I found myself trying to please other people, yet I was dying inside. I felt that because he had gotten away with so much, he had me in his hands. I will try to relate a few more incidents that I remember in the course of our three years together.

Chapter Four: Losing My Virginity

HIDING IN THE WARDROBE

Courage is being afraid but going on anyhow

—Dan Rather

Because of the many fights we previously had, I had secretly begun to keep a sharp long nail filer with me at all times. I knew I could not hit him back, so I planned to stab his hand any time he tried to hit me. So, on this occasion, as the argument heated up on the couch, I began to get irritated and took out the nail filer from my pocket and kept in my hand on my side. Even though I was upset, my hand was sweating, because I knew that something bad could happen to him. He raised his hand to smack me, but before he could even put his hands on me I took the nail filler and tried to stab him; I felt scared because the confidence that arose in me was out of this world. I felt big and not myself, and he leapt back and started shouting at me, accusing me of wanting to hurt him. *Hahahaha*, I had to chuckle, *so even the Goliath in front of me was scared.*

Honestly speaking, I was also terrified of my actions. I felt something I had never felt before, and because I didn't want to be beaten, I ran upstairs to the bedroom and hid myself in the wardrobe. I was so tiny then, but how he could open it repeatedly without seeing me crouched inside it is a mystery until today. I am sure that even his drunkenness left him, because he knew I ran away upstairs—but to not find a person, that is a miracle in itself. I could say that God keeps His own; whichever way it was on this particular night, I am grateful that I did not feel the pain of his hands on me.

BROKEN MIRROR BEFORE CHURCH SERVICE

Sometimes, I look at my scars and I see a girl who tried to cope with all the horrible things

—Unknown

One Sunday morning, whilst getting ready for church, an argument ensued because Saul accused me of spending too much time at church and I just lost it. I am not a morning person, so I was annoyed that he had started irritating me when I had just woken up. In anger and frustration, I lifted a mirror and hit my head repeatedly to get his attention and it broke into a million of pieces. How I did not cut myself is a mystery. The only way to explain this irrational behaviour is that I was now hopeless or crying for help in my own way, and I didn't realise that I was now hurting myself in desperation.

A lot of people, when they lose power or control over their bodies in life, they deal in self-harm behaviours, such as cutting yourself, or conditions like anorexia or bulimia. A person is not thinking in a rational way but trying to gain the control back. In most of these cases, when extreme, medication and rehabilitation help. It is important to ask for help when you realise just how deep in you are.

I still went to church that morning, and led the praise and worship. In every season we still need to praise God, right? Of course, that wasn't me physically because it's impossible—I am human, after all, not a superwoman.

After church, I went to Papa and Mama's house (Saul's spiritual parents) and stayed the whole afternoon. His guilty conscience should have been killing him, wondering what I was saying to his beloved parents. Mind you, he is

Chapter Four: Losing My Virginity

the one who introduced me to them, so I shouldn't have been tarnishing his image. The devil is a liar! He came to take me home when he was a bit high, and so on the freeway it began: 'You spend all your time in church, *blah blah blah*'. Probably, on this Sunday my mind had just had enough. I just opened the door in the moving car at 90km/hr on Reid Highway. I just couldn't stand it anymore and he had to stop on the side of the road. He told me off for wanting to get him arrested—did I have to go that far to make him stop irritating me?

As I reflect, I ask myself, *what I was doing to myself?* It is beyond my understanding. *Was it worth it?* Probably not. I had had enough of everything and just wanted to be away from him or just sleep forever. In as much as I could not think anymore of what I was doing, I feel that even those people who were around us and knew what was going on did not encourage me to leave him. I understand that a relationship is between two people and I needed to say it myself that I wanted out—it wasn't their responsibility. But I do not ever remember anyone telling me to leave Saul, and as a person who was used to having the elders tell me what to do, where to go and how to move, I was now in a place where there was no one to direct me. When I used to run to Mama and Papa's house, he would constantly ring and text, and they would tell me not to answer, but even then, I used to pick up the phone or read the messages, as I felt they didn't understand that the more I ignored him the more he kept ringing and texting. Saul was controlling me in the wrong way. Perhaps it was because I had met all the people close to me now through him, and they did not want to tarnish their friendship; I don't know. Perhaps it was because we were all Africans and this behaviour is tolerated in our culture.

CINDERELLA'S ONE SHOE STORY

Never look back. If Cinderella had gone back to pick up her shoe, she would never have become a princess

—Unknown

On another Sunday evening, whilst going back home from Mama and Papa's house, Saul was still complaining about me spending less time with him than at church. *Aaaaah, the stories and lies are the same.* We left the house, probably close to midnight, and just a few minutes into the drive we were shouting at each other, then he tried to slap me and I got mad and just veered to the side of the road. This would have been one of the worst accidents in Perth, as the car had lost control and went into a ditch. How I managed to get out of the car in tact but with only one boot on my feet is a mystery.

I ran back to Mama and Papa's house, but I had to pass through an open area field which had Xanthorrhoea trees around. Because I was scared he would catch me, I hid behind one of the big Xanthorrhoea trees I could see, as I did not want Saul to know where I was going. I laid flat on the ground, trying hard to hold my breath (as I had been running) and hid close to the shrubs. He passed me a few times, calling out my name. Those who know me well can testify I cannot stand cats, let alone snakes, and where I was hiding would have been the perfect place for such beautiful friends, but that never crossed my mind. The monster after me was more dangerous. It's just as well I had watched some action movies, for that moment in time I felt like a recruit in training, watching my enemy's every move.

He called after me and I just lay behind the shrubs till I realised he had left, then I ran to the phone booth close by and called Mama and Papa's house. Though I couldn't say much, they knew I was in trouble and came around looking for me. They found me walking back to their house. We got back

Chapter Four: Losing My Virginity

to the house and I stayed with them for some time till Saul came to take me back, and yes, I went back. I never reported this incident to the police. The following morning, I went with Papa to the ditch to look for my shoe and there was nothing except the wheel marks of the car.

I have to say, we were probably now good at our mind games—he would come and beg for forgiveness and I would go back to him. According to Cathy Spatz Widom (1989), there is factual evidence to support what psychologist Lenore Walker in 1979 found: that many violent relationships follow a common pattern or cycle. The model below was developed by Lenore Walker and is also used by domestic violence organisations in Australia. Looking at the pattern below and how our relationship was, this is so correct.

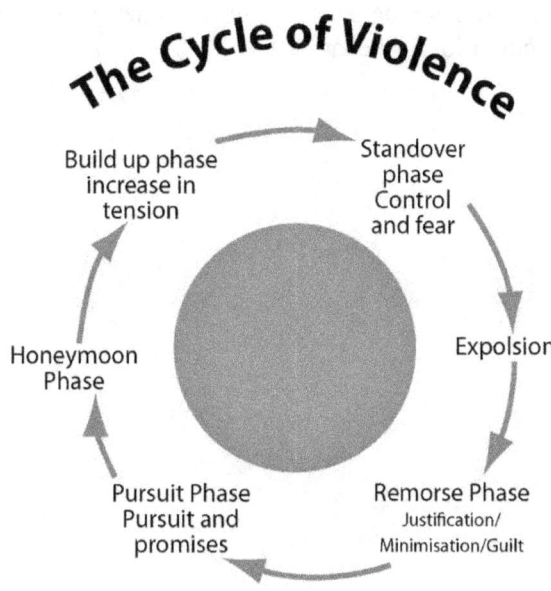

This map was developed by Olga Botcharova at
http://www.listugujhavenhouse.ca/learn/cycle-violence/

According to the Mayo clinic staff (2017), 'if you're in an abusive situation, you might recognize this pattern: your abuser threatens violence, your abuser strikes, your abuser apologizes, promises to change and offers gifts. Then the cycle repeats itself. The longer you stay in an abusive relationship, the greater the physical and emotional toll. You might become depressed and anxious, or begin to doubt your ability to take care of yourself. You might feel helpless or paralysed. You may also wonder if the abuse is your fault — a common point of confusion among survivors of domestic abuse that may make it more difficult to seek help.'

Looking back at his manipulative behaviour, he knew I did not hold grudges; he would give me space for a few weeks and let me calm down. After all, going back to Zimbabwe was not an option for me, so eventually I had to go back to him, as this was the condition of the visa. Saul was good with his tears: he could cry and apologise and promise to never touch alcohol again, as he accused alcohol for his behaviour.

Chapter Five

EMBARRASSMENT IN FRONT OF THE WHOLE CHURCH

A wolf is no less a wolf because he's dressed in sheepskin and the devil is no less the devil because he's dressed as an angel

— Lacrae

CHAPTER FIVE

EMBARRASSMENT IN FRONT OF THE WHOLE CHURCH

After more than a year and half of Saul never admitting to hitting me, and accusing me of being a drama queen who is after a permanent residence, I left Saul's house and went to stay with Mama and Papa for a while. Saul kept calling and asking me to come back home, to which I objected. We had a barbeque at Mama and Papa's house one Saturday and the whole church was invited. He also went to this church, so he must have been told that everyone would be in attendance. Whilst in the middle of preparing for this day, Saul came to have a talk and I remember I was sitting on the floor, busy peeling sweet potatoes.

He called me a few times to come outside and talk, but I didn't pick up the phone. He could call more than twenty times in a few minutes; they say men cannot text, but this man knew how to text very well. After every missed call, a text followed. Unknown to me, he had planned that if things didn't go according to his plan, he would leave all my clothes on the edge of the road, which he did. Not only this, he made two more trips to bring all my clothes and leave them on the lawn next to the main road. I wouldn't be surprised if this was another of his practical jokes to try and manipulate me so I would agree to come back. The first trip could be forgiven for a mistake—more than two trips means you know what you are doing. To add salt to this wound, he brought a set of white kitchen cutlery and put it on top of my belongings and left. How could a normal person behave in such a manner? He knew how to torment a person—after working tirelessly for the two years we lived together, was I worth only a set of white cutlery?

This did not only embarrass me in front of everyone, seeing all my undies out, but it was so shameful that I felt like I needed someone to dig a hole and bury me. Death could not come any quicker for me. After dropping off my

Chapter Five: Embarrassment In Front Of The Whole Church

belongings, then came the text messages and calls, but I knew this game too well and I didn't respond. The text messages really hurt, but I thank Mama and Papa for continuing to encourage me not to respond and to just let him be, even though this was not easy. When he eventually realised he had messed up and I wasn't returning, he came up with the mother of all plans.

One Sunday morning, Saul turned up at church and during the time of testimony he stood up to speak his mind. I wasn't interested in hearing anything, as I had heard all this before. Saul, for the first time, admitted his wrong doings and said that he had been beating me and asked for forgiveness, with tears too. He admitted that alcohol was also partly to blame for his behaviour and that from that day onwards he would not touch alcohol for the rest of his life, and that if he ever touched alcohol again the pastors or God should cut his hands off or something, as he intended to change. He said I was what he needed.

This is when we say, 'The Oscar for 2006 goes to … ' Most people in church were in tears and some were recording—it was mind blowing. Could he have won more people's hearts that day? It was so touching. I remember the lady who was seated next to me saying, 'Tinashe this man loves you, today just go back home.' Admittedly, I was also touched a little bit; he had never admitted to his narcissistic behaviour, so this was the real deal. After church, I packed my bags, except the set of cutlery, and I went back.

As they say, a leopard never changes its spots. The manipulative and narcissist person Saul was could not be hidden for too long. On the way home, with the whole church on his side (as he would have loved), he accused me of being too pompous because I had made him come and embarrass himself in front of the whole church. For crying out loud, did I put a knife over his throat and force him to come and confess his sins to the whole church? He had no shame whatsoever. As he was popular, he always wanted to keep his clean image at my expense.

MIGRAINE HEADACHES

The community is well aware of the physical aspect of domestic and family violence, but might be lacking understanding of all the other elements which include emotional, financial, psychological, property damage and technology amongst others. Because of this we are missing the early signs and opportunities to intervene before long term damage is caused to these families

—Domestic and Family Violence worker quote

Over the years, as I continued to be in the abusive relationship, my health deteriorated and I developed excruciating migraine headaches. If I had been able to chop off my head I would have, as it was unbearable. There could have been so many reasons, and the obvious was not eating. I could not have a decent meal in peace and I was always on the run. Even when I ate, it was just for the sake of it. When I first met him, he was so skinny and tall; after a few months of living together, he gained so much weight it was not funny. He could not fit his clothes, yet the opposite could be said of me. It is amusing that Saul occasionally threatened to end our relationship because I was not eating. And he constantly made the point that people will think he abuses me. How ironic. It always came back to his reputation.

Lack of sleep and anxiety could also have caused the constant migraines; my mind was working overtime, and I was always on the run—deteriorating health was inevitable. The headaches became so severe, I remember even Mama and Papa trying to research about migraines in books and all. Nightmares would soon follow; this was now a horror movie in real life, not that I have ever watched a horror movie.

Chapter Five: Embarrassment In Front Of The Whole Church

RUN-IN WITH DRUGGIES.

Not all dangers are obvious

—Leah Cypess

One night, we fought about something and I called the police. I thought I was lucky enough to escape and because it was freezing cold I could not go any further. I just knocked hard next door. I had never seen the people next door, but I just thought *let me try my luck before Saul could follow me*. Someone opened the door and I just snuck in and closed the door behind me before Saul got out of the house.

Little did I know that this would turn out to be an escape into the lion's den. After catching a breath, I opened my eyes and realised the house was full of young boys taking drugs and drinking. I just said hello and they looked at me, amused. I looked at my surroundings and there were cans of alcohol all over the table, white powder on the table and shisha tubes. No one asked me who I was or what I wanted, I was just offered a chair and I sat right behind the door.

I can only assume we were all high, that no one cared about anything else. I, on my own fear, and for them in a different world, high on their substance. Not only was I running from danger, but my abusive relationship made me vulnerable to these kinds of dangers. I could have been raped for all I know, but it didn't register to me at the time. I heard the police outside and Saul was talking to them and I heard him say, 'She always does this, are you not tired of her calls already. She is a drama queen seeking attention.' This would have been a perfect moment for me to get out and speak to the police, but I had no strength in me to stand up. I was just out of it. I called them for help and here I was, just numb. After a while I just stood up and said thank you and went back home. He asked me where I had gone to and I said I was next door. He told me to stop calling the police on him because he would eventually be arrested. Again, it always came back to protecting himself.

BOBBY'S CALL FROM THE UNITED KINGDOM

She's got the eyes of innocence, the face of an angel. A personality of a dreamer, and a smile that hides more pain than you can imagine

—Unknown

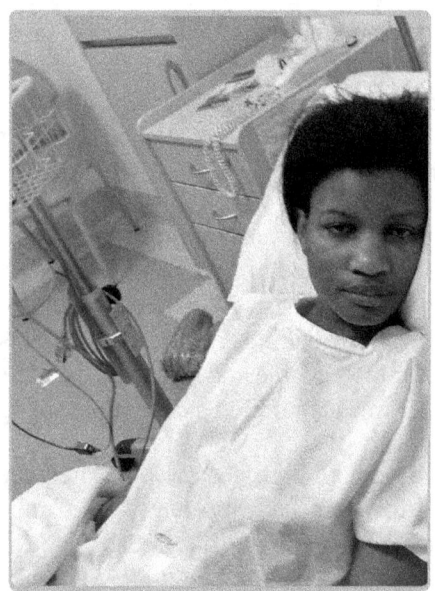

I had a guy friend, Bobby, who lived in the United Kingdom, and I had given him the landline number to ring me because there was nothing else to our relationship than being friends. Bobby called me on a Saturday afternoon and we had a lovely conversation whilst Saul was sitting on the couch having his favourite drink and watching TV. As I couldn't hear properly, I just took the landline handset and went out to stand on the balcony, leaving the flyscreen door ajar. As soon as I had finished my phone conversation, things turned 360

Chapter Five: Embarrassment In Front Of The Whole Church

degrees in a matter of seconds. I came back into the house and he smacked me right across the face and accused me of cheating. These cheating accusations never got old.

I tried to explain myself, and said, 'Would I be really that stupid to give a lover the landline number?' He replied, 'The way you were talking and giggling, anyone could tell you have been lovers forever, call him back so I can talk to him! I always knew that you were staying for my visa, and when you get it you will go to your lovers, sorry you have been caught, neither are you getting the residency but your UK boyfriend will also know you live with me today.' We continued arguing and fighting, and sadly enough, he hit the crap out of me. I tried to ring Mama and Papa, then Kiri and Mukoma to come and help, but he smashed the landline phone into the wall, and did the same with my mobile. He was throwing the washing basket, the clothes and anything he could find at me and screaming. 'You pretend to be innocent and now your true colours are coming out. I can't believe you were talking to your boyfriend right in front of me, you think I am so stupid? You slut.' I had no phone to ring anyone so I just cried. He took all the house keys, including mine, locked me in the house and left.

That day, I felt hopeless. No one was going to come and rescue me. We had a two-storey apartment, so I went downstairs into the lounge and calculated if I could jump downstairs from the balcony veranda. We lived on the second floor of the apartment building, but I didn't want to hurt myself. I was not confident I could jump that high and I also remembered he had taken the keys with him so I couldn't go outside anyway.

Because of the crying and hunger I had a migraine headache. Migraines had become a part of my life. On this particular day, my head was pounding; it felt like it was going to explode. I was so exhausted and I needed a peaceful sleep. So, I went into the bathroom and contemplated jumping out of the bathroom window, but again I did not have the confidence to do that. That very day I gave up on life. I felt that whether I died or not it was the same, so I took Panadol tablets—I don't know how many, because I wasn't thinking straight. On an empty stomach, those tablets reacted so quickly and I collapsed. Until today, I don't know if I was trying to kill myself, because a few minutes before I was scared of jumping out and here I was now, taking tablets.

When he came back he found me lying hopelessly on the bed or floor (I don't remember which), not responding, and drove me straight to the Princess Margaret hospital. I was told that the doctors checked me and told him I was still alive but told him to take me to Sir Charles Gardener Hospital, where I was subsequently admitted. What I felt that night was like nothing I felt before: I didn't want to close my eyes, as I felt like I was dying slowly. I couldn't feel myself; I was out of the real world. I felt life leaving me slowly and I kept beeping for the nurse. I give glory to God that among the many millions who have died of overdose/suicide, He kept me alive. Until today, I don't know what it is I was trying to do to myself—was it suicide or an overdose?

I remember feeling better the following morning, and Kiri and Mukoma came to visit and they were upset with me. I can't remember the full details of the conversation we had, but I remember them asking me if killing myself was really the solution. The social workers came that morning and interrogated me but I kept my mouth tight-lipped. One would think that this was the day I would finally confess to authorities and have this monster jailed, but I denied abuse or any form of violence. Eventually they gave up on me and I was discharged.

I felt scared to tell the authorities of what had happened because I knew Saul would be arrested. I did not want to be that person who dobs another person in and gets them imprisoned. I was afraid of the people we knew pin-pointing me to be the one who made one of theirs go to jail. I could not live with that burden. I protected the monster. In hindsight, I should have confessed everything to the social workers and not returned with him to the house because silence is not the solution, and the situation had reached a dangerous point.

Saul was so shaken and scared he drove me straight to Mama and Papa's house. He asked me if I had told anyone anything, and I said no. On our way,

Chapter Five: Embarrassment In Front Of The Whole Church

he told me that I was the evil one, trying to plot evil by killing myself. I was just out of it and just wanted to rest. Mama and Papa were not happy, as you can imagine. I remember them saying, 'What would we tell your mother if you had died?' Furious as they were with me, and as unfortunate as this was, I believe that this was the first time they actually believed that something was actually wrong with this relationship. It must have been hard for them to acknowledge that Saul was the one in the wrong, because to them he was the most outgoing, outspoken and fun-loving person out there. And yes, I met them through him, which he reminded me for the whole time I was with him. On this day, I managed to speak my mind and confessed to everything that had been going on. When I say everything, that included our sexual relationship, as at times it was forced, and at this stage I was not interested in it whatsoever. This infuriated him and was therefore a contributing factor to our relationship troubles. They encouraged me to keep talking and air everything out. Saul tried to interrupt me so I wouldn't air out all the dirty laundry, but they encouraged him to be quiet and let me finish first. His two-faced nature was brought to light and I think when I aired out our sexual relationship he realised that this was it, his evil nature was being exposed. This was rape being exposed too, but I was using kind words such as 'being forced'. I eventually went back to our place that night, as I always did, and things changed a bit because I had pulled out the best stance according to him.

I told Nicky what had happened and she had had enough of my stories and took me to Subiaco to see a lawyer. I met the lawyer and talked about my situation and everything that had been going on, and he advised me that I was not the only one going through this. He said I didn't need to continue in this relationship and that the visa that I was worried about was less important than my life. He advised that the government was aware of such kind of people and that they wouldn't just send me packing for Zimbabwe without hearing my side of the story. From memory, the services to help me with my visa issues would cost at least two thousand dollars. He told me that even though I didn't have this money, I could do a payment plan, as he thought I was in danger and needed to leave Saul. I was taking notes during this meeting and that was the first time I ever thought I could actually leave Saul. I was full of hope and confidence. All that I needed to do was to gather the evidence and file a case. When I got home I had to hide these notes somewhere Saul could not see, so I decided to put the notes under the mattress. As I always made the bed I thought he would never suspect anything to be under the mattress. How wrong was I? I don't know how, but one day he confronted me with the notes and accused me of plotting to tarnish his image. He told Mama and Papa that I had met with lawyers and honestly speaking, I didn't care what they thought of me then. Whether they believed his lies that I was just there for a visa or that I am the drama queen he claimed, I wasn't bothered as I had seen the light. He tore up my notes, but I knew what I needed to do. I didn't know where to start to gather the evidence, but I was a woman on a mission.

He went back to work a few weeks later, but he could not get over my confidence in meeting with a lawyer. I had stepped out of my comfort zone and had not consulted the people he knew, so he was scared. And to turn events around, he told me of how I was stressing his life and making him miserable—that he was going to take his own life and die that night. To make it more dramatic, he hung up on me.

We had just gone through an overdose a few weeks earlier and I had never heard him talk like this before, so I panicked and rang Mama and Papa and I asked them to ring him. I also rang the police in the north. Mama and Papa rang him, and according to them he was just pulling my leg, but I needed proof from the police that this was all his practical jokes again. Eventually, the police rang me back to give me feedback and they had found him drinking, watching soccer and having a good time. This incident just confirmed or provided further evidence that I was dealing with a manipulative person. I went through so much trouble and so many calls just for someone who was playing a prank on me. My life had become a joke to Saul.

According to Simmonds Publication, 'Manipulative people have a strong need to be in control. This may derive from underlying feelings of insecurity on their part, although they often compensate for these feelings with a show of strong self-confidence. Even though they may deny it, their motives are self-serving, and they pursue their aims regardless of the cost to other people. They have a strong need to feel superior and powerful in their relationships—and they find people who will validate these feelings by going along with their attempts at manipulation.' This theory describes perfectly the abusive behaviour of control and domination by Saul.

Chapter Six

LIFE CHANGING HOLIDAY

One day, you will wake up and there won't be any more time to do the things you've always wanted. DO IT NOW

—Paulo Coelho

CHAPTER SIX

LIFE CHANGING HOLIDAY

After all these dramatic events, a few months into 2007, whilst Mama was putting laundry out, she said she heard an audible voice telling her that Saul was not the one for me. So, she advised me to take a holiday to Zimbabwe and have a break. I decided to plan for a trip back home in December 2007 for a well-needed rest. And also to plan how I could eventually get out of this toxic relationship.

I told Saul I wanted to go home and he proposed that he travel with me. So, we booked and arranged our flights, with a week tour in Malaysia (Kuala Lumpur) before we returned to Perth. I was so excited to go back home to see my family; it would have been three and a half years since I last saw them, and this was going to be a good distraction for me. However, Saul could not travel to Zimbabwe for political reasons, so he was going to invite all his family to South Africa.

One Sunday evening, there was going to be a soccer game with Manchester United and all the boys were coming over to our place, as always. I prepared dinner for everyone and as it got late, I decided to go to bed as I was working early in the morning. I said my goodnights and went to bed. Little did I know that Saul was not happy. In the early hours of the morning when everyone had left, he came to bed and woke me up so we could talk. He asked me why I had behaved rudely by walking off in front of his friends, saying that I had shown displeasure of their company. I couldn't believe what I was hearing and I said bluntly, 'I went to bed because I was tired, it was late at night and I have work in a few hours for goodness sake.' He continued to argue and accused me of painting a bad picture of our relationship in front of people. I couldn't stand such nonsense, so I just went into the bathroom and locked the door and slept in the bath tub.

Chapter Six: Life Changing Holiday

After a few minutes, he came knocking so we could finish the conversation and I was not having any of this nonsense—I just lay in the bathtub so I could sleep. He started shouting and screaming because he thought I was going to commit suicide. I just ignored him and, before I knew it, the whole door and glass was down. He had broken the bathroom door. Probably because he was dead drunk, he did not feel the pain of breaking the door. I just went back to sleep and eventually he fell asleep too. We had to get a new door because of his unnecessary violence.

In the midst of all this, on August 9 2007 I started a new job, and I recall being asked if I had any holiday plans. I regrettably told my new boss I had already booked a six-week holiday to Zimbabwe in December. As I had already been offered the job there was nothing he could do and I was allowed to take leave. My life was chaos as it was—any more misfortunes would not have been welcome.

With my new job came a new challenge I had never experienced: racism. Even whilst I was preparing to come to Australia, my parents and the Koala agency we had used never prepared me for racism. I had been in Australia for three years and had studied and worked with white people without any problem, as far as I was concerned. In fact, when I applied for my first full-time job whilst I was still living with Cathy in November 2004, they told me they didn't employ women in general because it was a heavy lifting job. The warehouse was three minutes from my house and the money was good. I told the manager, 'Being an African girl and having worked in my parents' shop, I can handle this—try me first.' This job involved lifting twenty litres of oil, ten to twenty kilos of sugar, rice, flour, salt, etcetera. It was all bulk stuff. I got the job and thoroughly enjoyed working with the Caucasian men from different nationalities. This, for me, was an experience of a lifetime. I had never been into a freezer before, and here I was spending time in this cold room packing cheese, milk, feta and many other cold foods. I never saw colour or gender. Before I resigned, I am happy to say that they were at least three more women working there and we worked happily together.

So here I was now, in August 2007, in a different warehouse with a majority of Asian and white Australian workers. I started working with one white Australian woman who showed her dislike of me from my first 'hello' with a curt response. I just assumed she was having a bad day. After the first week, I could sense something was not right—if I was not careful she could have had a carton of shoes fall on me. She was deliberately careless, as cartons would fall on my side and just missed hitting my head. I would tell her off at times, and she was always rude in her responses: 'Why are you standing in my way then?' I confided in one of my workmates and he complained to the supervisor. She was moved to a different working area.

Before I knew it, we were once again packing shoes next to each other. She was just irritating in the way she handled her work area—it was just to push me over the edge. She would purposely pile shoe cartons dangerously high, not forgetting she was tall in height. So not only did I come to work with a heavy load on my shoulders from home, but here I was again, being bullied by the not-so-nice missy. I soon found out she was probably five years older than me, though she was way taller and huge. One busy morning, I irritated her so much that she just took a pair of shoes and threw it right at me. I was fortunate, as the shoe missed me by a few inches. I had not talked to her, as I never bothered to greet her anymore. The work area was at a standstill, as this was not called for. I went straight to the supervisor and reported her, only to be told, 'You know her, she is crazy. Since the shoes didn't hit you, just ignore her and continue with your work.' In my mind, I was screaming, 'Are you kidding me, someone just threw shoes at me for nothing.' What was I to do? I just let it slide and continued with my business, after all I was good at keeping quiet when abused.

One of my workmates (my husband now) wasn't having it, and told me to go and report to the manager as this was unacceptable behaviour. With a little encouragement, I went to the manager's office and reported the incident. To his surprise, the supervisor had not mentioned anything. However, his response as well was not convincing, 'I am sorry this happened to you, but can you let it slide for this time as this girl has a few mental issues. Working here is preparing her to be around people and get the experience.' What could

Chapter Six: Life Changing Holiday

I say after that? I actually felt sorry for her—after all, she wasn't well.

I did well with my work and, before I knew it, I was promoted. And you will not believe me if I say this, after my promotion this same girl who threw a shoe at me started greeting me: 'morning', 'afternoon', 'have a nice weekend', 'can I please have this', 'can I please order that', or in a conversation she would also put her 'two cents'. Even until today I am in shock every time she speaks to me. Did I have to be at a higher position than her to get her acceptance as a person worthy to converse with?

The very person who had referred me for the promotion soon realised I was too good at everything I did and I became her enemy. After working with her for a few months, one morning she came in the office and said, 'Is it just me or does this office smell like a toilet?' I don't know about you, but a toilet? This was just a few minutes before my boss and I had walked in. I had had a shower and put on a nice perfume. There is no way the tiny little office would have smelt like a toilet. I could only wonder if the nice comments the visitors kept making—'this office always smells nice'—could have been irritating her. From memory, she complained when people came in and only acknowledged me, as if she wasn't present. After all, she did not have a good reputation with everyone—without being rude she was called 'a female dog'.

I was fuming, deep down, so much that I could not concentrate on my work. To me, this was real racism, not based on ignorance, but a deliberate attack of my personality, trying to reduce me to nothing. On my tea break I rang Mama and told her what had happened that morning. As she was aware of a few things that had been happening, she told me to pack and leave for the day. I was afraid of walking out, as I didn't know what my rights were. I worked quietly till the end of the day and left. However, I did not go to work the following morning; I was still mad. It was the work policy to ring the head manager when you couldn't make it for work, not texting.

The fact that my boss heard everything from his office the previous day and did not comment or say anything was even more outrageous. So, I decided to be more outrageous and sent him a text message that I was not coming to work that day. I assumed he knew why I was not coming to work, so I never got his response. Mama told me to stay home for the rest of the week and ask for stress leave. Me being me, I was too much of a chicken. The following day I went back to work.

Later in the day, my boss called me into his office and confronted me for sending him a text message when I knew it was not permitted. I lied and said, 'I tried to call you initially, and then realised that I had run out of credit, but I could still text as I had a few free texts left.' I couldn't care less at this point. He went on to talk about the comment about 'the office smelling like a toilet' and he advised me that he had spoken to her the previous day and she would not do it again.

Honestly speaking, I didn't buy into it. That is the day I realised that I was just another worker and nothing more. I lost respect for the man for whom I had once had high regard, as I felt that he too was just being fake. A few things had been said and were happening inside the office, like being told off for no apparent reason, so for me this was the last straw. I knew that my workmate was intimidating and bullying me, but fear controlled me. As I reflect on one particular incident, my workmate didn't work on Fridays, so I borrowed her ruler from her desk as I couldn't find mine. I forgot to replace it and on Monday she realised her ruler was missing and she went off at people taking her stuff. I was scared to even admit it was me. I waited anxiously for my boss to get to work that morning. As soon as I saw his car I went downstairs to meet him before he came into the office. I dragged him into the kitchen and confessed to taking the ruler and forgetting to replace it. I asked him to lie that it was him who had taken this ruler so I wouldn't be told off. When my boss came into the office he went about his business, then I snuck the ruler onto his desk. After a while, he came and gave my workmate her ruler and apologised for not returning it. When I think of this incident I now realise that my fear of standing up to bullies has crippled me. This was just a ruler, but I could not even open my mouth to stand up for myself. What had started from a young age had grown with me into my adulthood and was now also affecting even the way I worked with others.

Chapter Six: Life Changing Holiday

However, I wasn't going to use racism to be an excuse to hate white people. Here I was, in a place where the majority are white; whether I liked it or not, I could not turn right or left without being surrounded by them. I decided to remind myself that my job was paying for my bills and I let it be, though it was not easy when I was seeing these people every day. Nevertheless, I refused to hate white people because of two people who had shown me dislike out of the hundreds I had met who respected me for who I was. Racism, from my own perspective—especially from my human context—is that it is a deliberate ideology orchestrated by those who want to feel superior over others, so that they can continue to enjoy certain privileges. It is lack of knowledge and understanding.

In Zimbabwe, the majority of people are black, however, all the white, Indian or Asian people I grew up around were as lovely as anything. If I met a different person I would be inquisitive to know about them, particularly if they greeted me in *Shona*, my mother tongue—then the conversation was even more exciting. I would usually ask how I greet a person in their language as well. I learnt how to sing a few songs in Bengali because I love music and I had some Bangladeshi friends. So, I just find it pure ignorance, arrogance and stupidity for someone to hate another human being or not accept them because of the colour of their skin. In this globalised age, I think this ignorance is selective because knowledge is so readily accessible; if one is interested in learning about others they can easily do that. I am more than my skin colour. If we were all the same, how boring would this world be? If being black was so horrible I am amused at why most white people love to tan nowadays. There is a lot that African/black cultures have given to the world which blows away the myth of black inferiority.

With an abusive boyfriend and a bully work environment, my holiday could not come sooner, I was indeed due for a detox. December came and we left Perth for Johannesburg. We got to South Africa and I had a few hours before my next flight to Harare so I met Thandie, the lady with whom Saul was going to stay in South Africa.

Eventually, I was on my flight to Harare late afternoon. It was just so beautiful and peaceful. The anticipation of seeing everyone was building up, and the nerves too. I was fearful of my family finding out I was living with a man in Perth as I had been living a lie all along. I had mixed emotions, to say the least. Upon arrival at the airport in Harare the joy on my family's faces was mind blowing. Everyone had changed so much; I left when my little sister was just a baby and here she was, almost taller than me with breasts coming out, and we were so alike. My younger brother was so big and tall—he lifted me up in the air like a balloon. On the other hand, my parents had lost weight and did not look so well; it shocked me, as I was not expecting to see this.

After visiting a few friends and relatives, it just hit me: that all these people thought I was having the time of my life overseas, yet they did not even know that I was living in hell and on the run every other night. Furthermore, 2007 had been a difficult year economically in Zimbabwe, hence I was not thrilled by the physical appearance of my family. Everyone else in my family, besides me, always had big bodies and for the first time they had lost so much weight. It dawned on me that I was working hard for someone who did not even appreciate me, yet I could have been giving my all to my family. I never mentioned any of my struggles to anyone in Zimbabwe—to me they were in a worse state than I was.

Whilst I was in Zimbabwe, Saul was in South Africa meeting his family as he could not travel to Zimbabwe. I had promised him I would travel to SA and meet his mum as he was planning on marrying me. Inside, I knew I could not visit him because I had no reason to give my parents. In Perth, I could do anything I wanted, but here I was back to their territory—how would I even dare to say, 'I am going to visit my boyfriend in South Africa'? Besides, as per Mama's counsel, I was working towards disengagement from this evil person. I never got to visit his family in SA and that, to him, was betrayal and an embarrassment. He had promised his mum his beautiful wife-to-be would visit. I talked to his mum occasionally on the phone whilst in Zimbabwe and yes, I had promised I would visit, but it never happened.

Chapter Six: Life Changing Holiday

Whilst on my holiday, I travelled to Botswana to get groceries and food items for my family because all the shops in Zimbabwe were empty. We had to stay overnight at a lodge close to the border, as it was a long journey, and we would resume the following morning. Early morning, we got ready and unfortunately there was no electricity, hence there was no hot water. I was used to having electricity 24/7 in Perth and here I was finding a new challenge in my motherland. There was no way I was having a cold shower (though everyone else had one), so I just washed my face and brushed my teeth.

We bought all we needed in Botswana and on our way back to Harare, we passed through Victoria Falls. My parents treated us to an overnight stay and I was relieved to finally have a warm bath—it felt like heaven. I soon realised that I was in a different territory. Whilst we were touring, a few police officers came close to the table that we sat at and accused me of stealing. According to them, I looked exactly like someone who had just stolen in one of the shops. I was shocked, but they had smelt a foreigner from afar and thought they could get a bribe. Thank God I had my family. The fire was put down quickly before the flames lit, and they apologised and continued walking.

We went to watch the Falls and honestly, I was just so happy to see my family happy. But all good things come to an end. When my holiday eventually came to an end, I picked up Saul in SA and we went to Kuala Lumpur in Malaysia. That time with Saul made me realise the urgency to get out of this toxic relationship. I never talked to or consulted anyone, I just made up my mind that this was it.

Firstly, even though the accommodation and breakfast had been paid for, he had spent all his pocket money. Had it not been for my mother we would have been penniless. At Harare International Airport I decided to give her the rest of the money I was left with and she said no, to use it in Malaysia. What angered me the most was that he had the audacity to get himself a gold necklace in South Africa and then come back empty handed. I thought, *what man was this always thinking of himself?* It just proved the narcissist he was: he only cared about himself.

Secondly, Malaysia is very humid and I got infected with thrush. At that time, I did not know what it was, I was just itchy and scratching. Beyond my belief, Saul had the nerve to accuse me of sleeping around when I was in Zimbabwe; to him, that was the reason why I did not go and visit him in SA, and here I was now, spreading AIDS (Acquired Immune Deficiency Syndrome) to him. This guy knew exactly where to hit my buttons. That was absolutely hurtful as he was the only man I had ever slept with my whole life. If anyone was to be accused of cheating it should have been him. He was staying in South Africa with a woman friend I knew nothing of, but I trusted him and never questioned this arrangement. So, as you can imagine, my Malaysian holiday could not end any quicker.

As soon as I landed back in Australia I did not care whether I was going to lose my spouse visa, *enough was enough*. Crazily enough, my permanent residence was due to be approved in five weeks' time. I had suffered for two years on a spouse visa and I wanted to get out as soon as I could. I had made up my mind, and there was no one stopping me from leaving him. Anthony Robbins once noted that, 'There is a powerful driving force inside every human being that once unleashed can make any vision, dream, or desire a reality.'

Because I knew how violent and crazy he could be every time I talked of leaving, I made up a plan of how I would leave without risking my precious life. I told Mama and Papa I was done with this toxic relationship. They asked me a few times if I was sure, as this was the first time they ever heard me talking; I was done. They were pleased with my decision and told me they had been waiting for such a long time to hear me say this with my own mouth. I confirmed I was sure and we decided I could not live with them as he would come and try to cause chaos. Once the plan was ready and I had found a place to rent, I told him before he left for work on the 9th of January 2008 that I was leaving him.

Instead of him finding an empty house, I thought *let me not be a coward*. He might have mistreated me but I was also grateful that he had helped me when I needed help the most. As expected, he did not take too kindly to my decision

Chapter Six: Life Changing Holiday

and started accusing me of giving him AIDS, shouting at the top of his voice so the neighbours could hear.

He said I had used him for a visa and that is why I was leaving now, as I was about to get what I wanted all along. He expressed that I had embarrassed him in front of his mum and daughter and everything under the sun that you can think of. Saul had a daughter who lived with his mum in Zimbabwe. The argument heated up, as I was denying all his claims, shouting at the top of my voice too. When I realised I was in trouble, I took the landline phone to call the police and he grabbed it and smashed it in the wall; this was neither the first, second, nor third landline that had been smashed into the wall, so it was no surprise.

I rushed to the bedroom to get my mobile phone and I rang triple zero and managed to say a few words—'my boyfriend is hitting me'—to the police on the other line. Saul grabbed my mobile and smashed it into the wall, and the last words I remember him saying, and I quote, were: 'You are ringing the police on me, by the time they come to arrest me and put me in prison you will be dead.' The anger on his face told me it was now or never. I tried to run out of the house, but he was too strong for me, and I remember trying so hard to push him away that I tore the t-shirt he was wearing. He was hitting my head and my hands, as they were covering my face, until he pushed me to the floor in one of the spare bedrooms. My leg hit the corner of the metal bed, tearing my ankle—gosh, that was painful—and blood gushed out. I don't know where I got the strength from to stand up and run, but I made it to the neighbour's house (who happened to be the landlord of our rental property). The wife nursed my leg whilst we waited for the police and once I heard the sirens I knew this was it for me.

I had never faced the police before, as I used to ring and run—by the time they arrived I was usually gone. This day, I remembered the words from the lawyer: to stop running when I called the police and truthfully tell the police what was happening, as it was their job to protect me. To those in Western Australia, the main piece of legislation relating to domestic and family violence is the Restraining Orders Act 1997. People need to learn to have confidence in the government system and dial that phone number, 000; it is free of charge. The police are there for us and they will protect us.

They were a few curious people standing around the street. I came out with my head high to the police and they asked me if I was the one who rang triple 000 for an emergency and I said, 'Yes it was me, I just told my boyfriend I didn't want to be in this relationship anymore, and because he was not happy about my decision he decided to hit me and that is how I have hurt my ankle as he pushed me to the corner of the bed.'

One of the police officers asked, 'Is all this blood in the driveway coming from your leg?' They were writing whilst we were talking, and the other officer went to speak to Saul whilst I went into the house with the other officer. As I was limping, the officer asked, 'Are you okay or do you want us to call the ambulance?'

I explained that I was okay and just wanted to finish packing my clothes.

They said, 'Do you know that it's a crime that he has committed, to assault you? You can press charges and we can take him with us to the police station for further questioning.'

'All I want is to leave him, can you please protect me from him?'

As mentioned previously, in Western Australia, the principal legislation relating to protection orders in the domestic violence context is the *Restraining Orders Act 1997* (WA) (the WA Act), supplemented by the *Restraining Orders Regulations 1997* (WA) (WA Regulations). Silly me, right? He deserved some time locked up! That is how sometimes being naïve and too kind will end up with most of us dead prematurely.

'We can give him a restraining order, how much time do you need to pack?' asked the officer.

Chapter Six: Life Changing Holiday

'I just need twenty-four hours and I will be done. By tonight I will be out of here, thank you so much.' I started sobbing from just the feeling of relief. I felt so good inside, I don't know why I made myself to suffer for so long. He denied hitting me, but the trail of blood from the front door into the driveway was evidence enough, and the police went to speak to the landlord next door.

They gave him a restraining order for 24 hours so I could pack and leave. He was forbidden from communicating or attempting to communicate by whatever means. The officers told me to report him if he ever tried to contact me or if anything else happened.

'And where are you going to, mate?' he was asked.

'Work, and I am already late as it is,' Saul said.

He broke the restraining order, because less than an hour later he called. 'So, you called the police on me, couldn't we sort out our differences without involving other people? Now I have a bad record on my name. So where are you going to stay? Can I come and we talk about it, I am so sorry Tinashe, I didn't mean to hurt you in any way.' On any other day, I would buy his tears and words but once I made up my mind I was not going backward.

The legislation states that 'It is an offence to breach a VRO (including a police order), with a maximum penalty of 2 years imprisonment or a $6000 fine, or both (s 61)'. However, I did not bother to report his violation of the restraining order as I thought that I would never see him again. Reflecting on this, I should have reported him to the police because for him this was the beginning of his revenge.

I packed my clothes and left that night to a share house that no one knew about except Missy Trish, Mama and Papa, Kiri and Mukoma. This share house was fully furnished, with five bedrooms, a kitchen, a lounge and a single toilet and bathroom. We all shared general cleaning duties equally; each person bought their own groceries and cooked for themselves, as well as cleaning after themselves. I was paying a hundred and fifty dollars a week including all bills (electricity, gas, water and Foxtel). Besides myself, there was another Sudanese girl, as well as Asian, Australian and Sudanese guys living with us. We were all so different and it was fascinating.

I found this share house in the weekend newspaper. I had to find a place that would suit my circumstances, and that was close to the bus station for easy transportation to work. I looked for an area close to my work as I needed to get on a bus for a 6.30 am shift. I needed a fully furnished house as I had little other than the clothes on my back. It was the best decision I ever made, but I had never imagined the emotional turmoil I was about to go through. After settling into my new surroundings, I was nervous and kept my phone with me, as I was expecting Saul to turn up at the front door, which never happened. Being alone in the bedroom on the first night reminded me I was now alone, and I broke down and cried for most of that first night and many more nights to follow. I was scared to face the following morning as I was paranoid that I would find Saul waiting for me on the side of the street, which never happened.

When I left Saul, Mama advised me to leave everything: the laptop, car, furniture, and to just carry my clothes only. I did not understand at first but now I understand why—I had nothing connected to him. This was a total fresh start to my life. What I have today cannot be even be compared to what I left behind. I have no regrets whatsoever.

I had just met Missy Trish a few months before and she was the best thing that could have ever happened to me. God will never leave you as an orphan. He gave me a big sister, just in time. She made sure to pass by the house almost every day and made sure I had eaten and I was okay. I remember that even at night after she had finished her late-night shift at 9 pm or 10 pm she would go to her house, make food and bring me something to eat. What kind of love is this? This was an angel from heaven, I love her to death. I remember even the times I needed transport, before I bought my car, she would come and pick me up, then I would drive her to her place and use her car to move around. She brought so much joy and naughtiness to my life—good naughty.

Chapter Six: Life Changing Holiday

Okay, I admit bad naughty too, but it was all good. We went out for dinners, movies, parties, concerts; I remember going to Rottnest Island on a boat for the first time for her birthday and my first time to see Celine Dion live was all because of her. We did so much in a few months that I often wondered which world I was living in before. It was a beautiful time and a deserving phase of my life, but I still had many demons to face inside me.

The fear of meeting Saul was always there, and I met him at a few concerts, but thank God, he never dared to come to me. I feared him turning up one day to the share house, which never ever happened. He visited and called my family friends, friends and church pastors and abused them when they would not be open with him about my whereabouts. He could have visited my workplace, but I thank God, he did not, because my boss was also ready for him. He could have stalked me from work to the place I was staying, but I thank God that never happened too. So, at times the things you fear might not even happen, as in my case.

Days and weeks passed after I had left. It was a scorching summer, as always, in Perth. The regret of leaving my car would arouse anger in me because I had to catch a bus when I knew he had my car sitting in his garage. At times, I was asked to stay back at work and work overtime, but because I had no transport it was difficult. That is how I met my husband, as he offered me a lift so that I was able to work overtime and save more money. Saul's text messages and phone calls were a nuisance, and guess what? I did not change my number. Mama advised me not to and said how would I know I had conquered my demons or weaknesses if I ran away from trouble. I faced it; it was a matter of putting my phone on silent and not answering the messages, and they became evidence to the police and immigration.

2008 was the time of *Hi5 (this was a social networking and media site for connecting with old friends and making new friends)*, before Facebook. And because I left my laptop with him, after the break-up I suffered sleepless nights, anxiety, depression, anger, shame—you name it—all because he changed all my online passwords on emails and everything. Saul hacked into my emails and chats on *Hi5*, writing on my behalf to all my male friends pretending to be me—these were filthy and dirty messages. He went on to call my mother in Zimbabwe. Every day, I woke up to calls from all over the world asking me what had got into my head for writing filthy posts on *Hi5*. On Monday the 25th February 2008, Ray, a high school friend, forwarded me the email below that had been sent to him by Saul pretending to be me on Saturday the 23rd February 2008:

I hope you still love me like I used to. I miss you like hell and I hope you are feeling the same way too. I was trying life in Australia here and I almost got there but Saul has found my trick and has cancelled his sponsorship. I have you as my last hope and if all fails here in Australia, I will join you in South Africa. I can't wait to make love to you straight away. Reply my mail because I am going through a tough time at the moment and I need your support. If everything had gone according to plan, you were going to join me because I was planning to leave Saul after I get the permanent residence in Australia. Remain sweet and I will be seeing you sometime soon.

Aka Tinashe

I almost collapsed when I read this, as I could not comprehend how Saul could write up such an email to a friend whom I respected. This was fraud. This was my worst nightmare (but real one) and beyond my control, but I thank God that Nicky introduced me to the cyber police, whom I never met, but I told them my story and everything changed. How they blocked everything, I don't know. I vowed to never touch social media again. I never even had the desire to join Facebook because of fear but now 'I'm no longer a slave to fear. I am a child of God' (Bethel Music). Being a child of God, the scriptures tell me God has not given me a spirit of fear and here I am today, connected to Facebook, Snapchat and Instagram with a sound mind.

In conclusion, if anyone finds themselves in a similar position as myself and has a source of income, they can find shared accommodation in the newspaper and online under rental properties. If you have no source of income there are shelters across the state that are open to accommodate you. You can find them online or the police can help you.

Chapter Six: Life Changing Holiday

Comparing then and today, technology-facilitated abuse has increased, as there is cyber bulling and luring. Back then, I had seen hacking in movies and never thought I would have an ex-boyfriend hack into my emails. With many more young girls like myself nowadays using digital technology I encourage them to be very careful. According to the Australian Bureau of Statistics' *Defining the data challenge for family, domestic and sexual violence, 2013*, 'Technology facilitated abuse means the use of digital technology to threaten, harass, monitor and control another person remotely. Examples include tracking via mobile phone apps, monitoring through the access of online bank accounts, threats to the partner via social media. Technology facilitated abuse is often linked to stalking as they may occur together.'

Chapter Seven

IMMIGRATION REVISITED

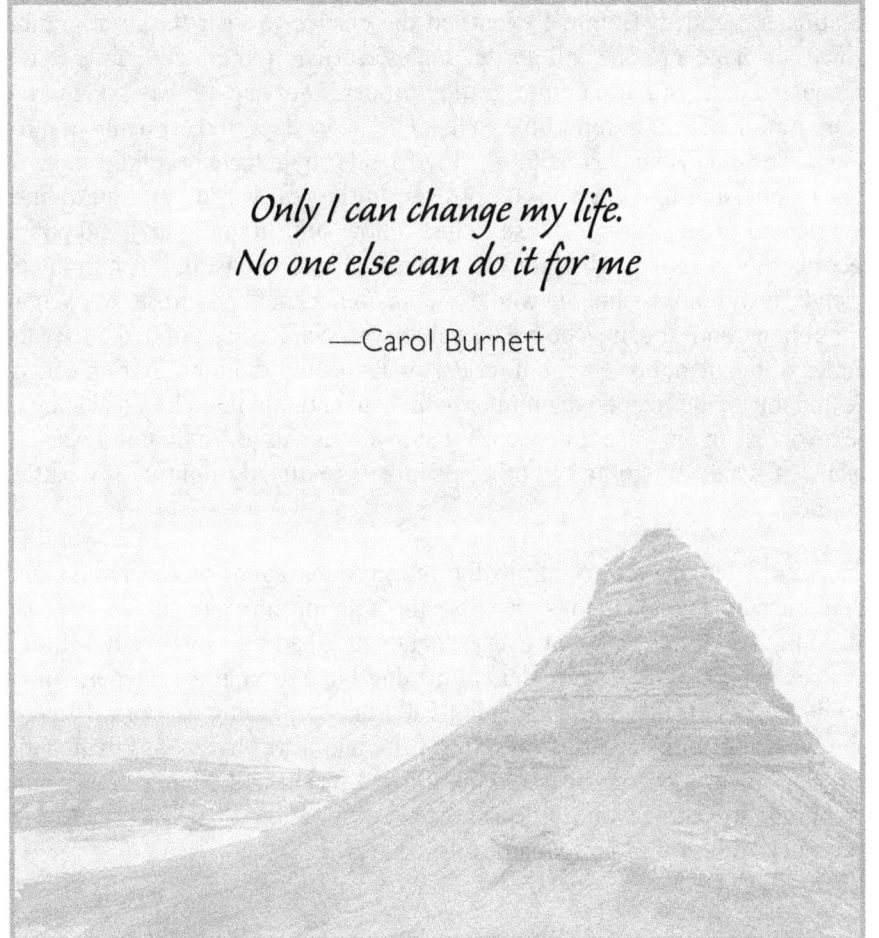

*Only I can change my life.
No one else can do it for me*

—Carol Burnett

CHAPTER SEVEN

IMMIGRATION REVISITED

Going back to the spouse visa issue, I had to deal with the immigration because the visa condition was to report to the officials as soon as the relationship ended. Before I even had the chance to visit the immigration offices or make a phone call, Pastor James, a friend I knew, called me to tell me he had met Saul at the immigration offices. Saul had already gone to the immigration offices to report me so that I could be deported for using him for a visa. The emails he was writing to my friends could have been his evidence that I was using him for a visa, however, in the real world you don't abuse people and expect everyone else to just follow suit. In my case, I had police records, journals, neighbours' testimonials, many pastors' testimonials, friends' testimonials, and the whole church and hospital records to prove how tumultuous and abusive the relationship was. Saul had confided in Pastor James of his plan, however, before Pastor James left the immigration offices he told me he left his phone number with them and told them he was happy to be a witness in our case if needed. What love was this, even though I was not aware of what was going on, other people were already fighting my battles for me.

Eventually, I managed to talk to the immigration agent on the phone, and he requested evidence to show that the relationship had ended because of domestic violence. I sent every document I had and just waited until I received a phone call a year later confirming I had been granted a permanent residence. As all this was happening I did not stop going to work, I took a bus every morning and cried myself to work and it was hard, but I thank God for the Grace upon my bosses who allowed me to call Mama. She would encourage me and I would finish the day's work and go back home. After a few weeks of saving I bought a beautiful car.

Chapter Seven: Immigration Revisited

Mama, in passing, had mentioned joining a karate class, so I joined a Taekwondo class close to work in Malaga. I had bought the movie Enough, which starred Jennifer Lopez, and I watched it so many times and it encouraged me to seek revenge, because I had never ever sat down to reflect on my life. Regrettably, I realised, I had made Saul trample over me, beat me, abuse me and let him get away with it. *Did you just realise it now Tinashe?* I would always ask myself. Even to you also reading this book, are you also realising now you are in an abusive relationship, or is your daughter, sister, friend or cousin? I felt then that now was the time to go back and do what I did not do before. *Revenge.*

These negative thoughts about revenge kept playing on my mind. The more I pondered these thoughts the more relief I felt that he had to taste his own medicine in an unexpected manner. Saul was a massive soccer fan, so I planned to go back to the house when all of his friends were gathered and enjoying themselves. With my newly acquired Taekwondo skills I was ready to release my anger and kill them all, to burn the house down—or so I thought. After all, I had bought some of the furniture, not just that set of white cutlery. I am happy to say I don't harbour such feelings of anger and revenge towards Saul today. I truly hope that he gets help, because I feel something is definitely not right. I am sure he also has a version of himself in this story. A few of my friends still hate him today, and I actually want them to forgive him and let it go, as this is not of any help to them or myself. I am really happy. *Happy* doesn't even do justice to the way I feel.

Three years ago, on the 5th of June 2014, as I was studying for my university examinations in my study, I just felt at peace and so happy that I started composing a song to reflect how I felt. The song goes something like this:

This joy, I never felt before, it makes me just want to dance

This walk I've never walked before, it washes away all my fear

This laugh, I've never laughed before, it washes away all my pain

Oh lord, I just want to say thank you, for all these feelings I'm feeling.

I got up and started dancing, using the table as a drum, and remixing it. I was laughing and crying—I didn't know what to do with myself. In a nutshell, that is how happy I am today.

When I left Saul in 2008, I was so disappointed with most of the friends I thought I had. Not even one of them rang to check and see where I was or what was going on. Eventually, after meeting a few people, I realised that some had been told I had used Saul for a visa and had been deported back to Zimbabwe. I knew Saul had a daughter and talked to her occasionally on the phone. I eventually met her when I went to Zimbabwe in 2007. I was surprised when I met a few other people who Saul had told that I had run away. Saul told these friends that I had left him because I found out that he was a father and I didn't want to be a stepmother. I knew of his daughter from the beginning of our relationship, as he mentioned he was a dad. So, I was hurt that here he was damaging my reputation with lies. I was upset with everyone, but I also came to the realisation that not everyone who smiles with you is for you. I cooked *sadza*, our traditional meal, for so many people in Perth, as our house was the party place. And most of these people knew what I was going through, but none dared to even check if I was okay or alive. If there is anything I learnt, it is the psychological ability to read people and understand their motives. As of today, I don't have many friends, but the few that I have are enough. Through my experience, I learnt not to rely on people to save me from my miseries or troubles—I need to help myself.

Chapter Seven: Immigration Revisited

FINES THAT NEEDED MY ATTENTION!

If you want to fly, you have to give up the things that weigh you down

—P. Diddy

The struggle is real. I found myself in unnecessary debt because of Saul without even realising it. As I mentioned earlier on, I left my car with him when we separated. In addition, his car was also in my name, as he had lost his licence. He did not pay the car registrations and accumulated fines using those cars as they were in my name. The bills that were in my name were not paid for. As the government system works, if your name is on it, it is your duty to pay for them. I had more than five thousand dollars' worth of bills to pay that were not my responsibility. As if that was not enough, I lost my licence due to unpaid fines.

The consequence of all this, I made payment plans for these bills to be paid. I have to admit that it really hurt me to the bone, but that it was my fault as well. Regardless of how chaotic my life was then, I should have also planned to take my name off the bills and car registrations. There are so many people like me or in even worse situations, paying thousands of dollars of debt for their boyfriends or girlfriends. This money could have gone to something better in my life, or to my family, but because I was so caught up in this disorder I ended up on the wrong side of the law. Whenever those alarm bells regarding finances were ringing in our relationship I should have asked for someone else's opinion or help, as my intuition was right.

Saul was smart and knew how hard working I was, otherwise he would not have chosen to be with me. We had constantly fought in the course of our relationship over finances because I felt like he was trying to live up to a certain image (party lifestyle) that he could not afford. Alcohol and spirits were not cheap, and as we were providing for the whole city, there definitely was not any money left for our savings. As a result of my complaining, I was always on the wrong end. I have learnt through my experiences to be cautious of any financial dealings with anyone. If my name is on it, I have to know what is on every dotted line because if I can't be responsible with my finances, I will consequently pay the price.

NIGHTMARES THAT FOLLOWED

Everything you've ever wanted is on the other side of fear
—George Adair

Even though I was going through good changes, something unwelcome popped up: I began to have nightmares. Initially, whenever I watched domestic violence scenes on the television or movies I used to get so emotional and I could actually feel the pain of the characters, even though it was not me. With time this went away, so I was excited to be living by myself and having my own space by 2010. Sleeping time became a horror movie interval—I would dream of dark black men almost every day, coming into my house through every opening in the house. Be it through the key holes, doors, the holes on sockets, the air vents of the house—anywhere you can think of that has a hole—these men wanted to come through it. On the lawn in front of my house there were always dark-skinned people waiting to get inside the house. It was scary. I felt people coming into my bedroom at night and I would fight them; it was not easy. I would dream of every male person I knew always wanting to rape me. Every time I met these people I was always anxious they would rape me. It was a dark place to be.

When these nightmares started, every time I had a bad dream I would always call the police for help in these dreams. Probably it's because I always thought that was the point of call when in trouble. In the real world I could call the

Chapter Seven: Immigration Revisited

police for help when I needed them, but in the spiritual world what were the police officers going to do for me?

Author, Scott Shaper, stated that, 'As you can see, domestic violence is a control issue. Actually, the psychological damage done by this type of behaviour is much greater than the actual physical abuse. Domestic Violence has no boundaries; it affects all levels of income. I had a one case where the domestic abuser was an educated male who made a six-figure income. His victim (former live-in girlfriend) was an educated female who made a nice income herself. They both had good jobs, and lived in an expensive condo. Well he had beaten her so badly that she was hospitalised with a closed head injury. Talking with her later she stated that she could not believe she found herself in this situation. She stated that her abuser was a white-collar worker who actually appeared on the outside to be a harmless geek. In fact, her friends couldn't believe he was capable of this. A few days later we were called back to the residence to stand by as peace officers, while the woman packed up her stuff and moved out. During the time that we were there, I noticed how she couldn't stop trembling. She was so afraid that her abuser would come back, and attack her while she was there. This was in spite of the fact that two Police Officers were with her the whole time (remember this was many days later). What is sad, this was not the first time she was abused, but hopefully with her leaving it will be the last. In case you're curious, yes, he was arrested.'

In July 2011, I travelled to Zimbabwe and I went to visit the lion and cheetah park in Norton while sightseeing with my parents. That very night I could not sleep; it wasn't the dark-skinned people after me, it was the lions. I just assumed it was because I had seen lions that day so it was not that much of a big deal. Then, interestingly enough, I went for prayers before I returned to Perth. As soon as I knelt down to pray, someone told me I had been having nightmares, and I was like, *Finally God is aware of my situation I am not just going crazy.* He prayed against the powers of darkness and rebuked everything that was coming against me, and I didn't think much of it afterwards. A scripture in Ephesian 6:12 says, 'For we are not fighting against flesh-and-blood enemies, but against evil rulers and authorities of the unseen world, against mighty powers in this dark world, and against evil spirits in the heavenly places.' When I returned to Perth I noticed a big change, though I still had a few gut-wrenching nightmares. As mentioned before, when I had nightmares in my sleep I would call the police for help in the dream because that's where my hope and trust was placed. When I woke up, I would realise that it's just a dream and no police would hear me in my bedroom. But after coming back to Perth, instead of calling the police in the middle of the dreams or nightmares I started calling the name of Jesus. I would now randomly have nightmares but I would call the name Jesus for help and, as this continued, I started praying in my dreams whenever I dreamt of something bad.

This became a part of me; I would dream and pray myself out of those situations—unconsciously, of course. And I grew stronger in my faith and became bolder. I wasn't scared to go to sleep, turn off the lights or have bad dreams, I just realised I had more power over the work of the devil. As this continued, I gained more trust in the Lord and I started dreaming of other people: family members, church members, pastors, people I meet daily or work colleagues— even the (back then) President of the United States, Barack Obama, and his family. I even started dreaming of people before they called me the night before, so that I would be aware of their intentions. This also improved my psychological ability to read people and understand their motives. At first, I didn't know what to do, and someone told me I needed to pray for these people I was dreaming of, so I would wake up and pray for the situations or against the situations. I feel God was helping me to overcome my fear of people.

I am now mostly aware of situations that happen in my life and my surrounding way before they happen. I am not easily surprised by the bad things that happen because I see them in the dreams before they manifest physically. What would have scared me or made me quit now makes me fight. I just know which battles I need to fight for. Not a physical fight, but a spiritual fight, because I know that is the plan of the devil: to kill, steal and destroy, as mentioned in John 10:10, 'The thief comes only to steal and kill and destroy. I came that they may have life and have it abundantly. I am the good shepherd. The good shepherd lays down his life for the sheep.' So greater is He who is in me than who is of this world.

Chapter Seven: Immigration Revisited

A word of encouragement from me is that there are some things that are beyond you, as these nightmares were to me. I didn't know why, who and where they were coming from. Some of you might be going through a similar situation or one that is different to mine; maybe you see that person who abused you coming at you at night and all you need is deliverance but you cannot deliver yourself. Go and look for help somewhere, and whoever helps you is not to be your god, as they are just a helper or vessel.

We are living in a generation where people worship palm readers, witchcraft, psychics, tarots, prophets and prophetesses and, I have to say, people need to wake up. As I am around many people, I see these things happening. These people are only there to warn you and help you in certain situations spiritually, not for you to become lazy and expect them to be your brains. The man who prayed for me never asked for a dime for his prophecy—freely he received the revelation and freely he gave it. I am not going back and forth to Zimbabwe to get more anointing or prophecies from him; he did his part, and the one who started the work in me had finished. I am free of nightmares, indeed. I would advise people seeking help to be careful and wise of the people out there, who are there to take advantage of your sufferings and weaknesses for their own sakes. Unfortunately, we are living in such times where exploitation and hypocrisy are at their peak.

It reminds me of one of the elders who knew what I had been through and knew how vulnerable I was. He is married with a family but took advantage of my brokenness and called me a few times to check up on me. That would have been great, however, the phone conversations turned to something else, as one day he told me to come and visit him in the countryside where he worked so I could get some fresh air and meditate. The alarm sound rang so loudly! I thought to myself, *If you want to help me, why should I visit you alone, when your family is not even there? Does your wife know about me and my situation?* So be careful of those who come in the name of help yet are there to benefit from your sufferings.

TOTAL TRANSFORMATION

First say to yourself what you would be; and then do what you have to do

—Epictetus

From my experience, seeking revenge was not freedom, as this was going to create a chain of troubles. As I mentioned earlier, I was going to assault Saul and his friends and burn the house down. Had I done this, I would have been arrested for assault or probably murder and destroying a property that did not belong to me. That would not have been freedom.

I could not control how I felt then and I was not capable of helping myself. I knew I was capable of being free from the past if I sought the help I needed and forgave the past and, most importantly, forgave myself. Carrying all the anger and frustrations of this world on my shoulders made me more miserable, particularly trusting other people who did not have my best interests at heart. I felt like the past was most likely to repeat itself so I created mechanisms in my mind to avoid such situations. I have been told that I could not smile, let alone laugh, at the funniest joke in the room. I met my husband at work and he told me once that he would greet me in the morning and I would not respond.

As many times as I have heard this, I still cannot believe that I would ignore people, because the person I am today loves people so much. I cannot relate to that Tinashe they talk about. So, this misery was not only a hindrance to my own growth but to others' as well. I call it 'a time bomb waiting to happen'. These days, we are more familiar with circumstances where people just randomly kill, run over and stab innocent people because of what has been done to them previously, or their families, tribes, religion and countries, etcetera. I could have easily been one of those people as I was out of my mind.

Chapter Seven: Immigration Revisited

It has always been my heart's desire to meet Pastor Robert Kayanja from Uganda. I had watched him over the years on videos and I pledged to visit Uganda to see him face to face. As fate would have it, God had other plans. On 1 October 2008, Pastor Robert came for a three-day conference in Perth. I was not missing this, and so I went. I was not going for anything in particular, it was just to see him personally because I thought that he was an amazing human being. Pastor Robert sang this chorus by Keith Green: 'I want to take your word and shine it all around. But first help me to just, live it Lord. And when I'm doing well, help me to never seek a crown. For my reward is giving glory to you.' This song has stuck with me for all these years; for the past year, as I have been writing this book, the lyrics keep reminding me of why I am writing it. I have lived every word I have written, and I just want to bring awareness about domestic violence and abuse.

I went to this conference faithfully for the three days and on the last day, he prophesied to a young woman in the audience—probably my age then—that she had had a difficult upbringing and was having a not-so-good life. On this particular night, according to the prophecy, God was going to reveal Himself to this girl and erase her painful past, and she would start a new peaceful life with so much joy.

Hang on a minute, is what I thought. *So, God can only see the suffering of this one girl, and how about me? Don't I deserve peace and joy too? So, you are a God of favouritism?* I am happy to admit I was livid. So, when Pastor Robert started praying for this girl, every word he spoke, I spoke the very same words to myself—talk about faith in action. I didn't even know what I was doing or what drove me to do that and if it would have any effect, but it worked. I remember in his teachings that night he said, 'Christianity is when God comes to you'. I prayed myself out of bondage and oh yes, God came to me. Proverbs 18:21 says, 'Death and life are in the power of the tongue, and those who love it will eat its fruits.' Through my experience, no one was going to help me face my demons. Not even my family in Zimbabwe knew what I was going through—no doctor, counsellor or pastor. The first step needed to be taken by me because I was the only one who knew how hot it was in this fire. I was sick and tired of feeling sick and tired. People could only sympathise with me, but I wanted to come out of this shell. I had tasted a bit of the good life.

After praying, I just fell on the chair. I don't know why I fell, because no one touched me, but I believe the Holy Spirit should have. Eventually, they took me to the front and he prayed for me but it was done already. This was the beginning of a new life for me and he also preached that 'God pulls you out to take you in'. After the conference was done and I had gone back to the share house, I just felt the urge to write a letter to Saul and send him a Christmas card. Mind you, I am always writing. I have been a writer for as long as I can remember, so this was nothing strange, letting all my feelings be known on paper. But writing a letter to Saul was strange. There is no way that in my right mind I would have thought of this. As mentioned earlier, I was going to Taekwondo so that I could beat the crap out of him, so this had to be something more than just me. There is a song that I love to sing, *It's no longer I that liveth, but Christ that liveth in me*. This was the beginning of God healing me and undoing all that happened to me.

In due course, Saul called when he received the letter, and I remember very well the sound of his voice when he asked a few times if it was really me who had written this and if I meant it. I would be surprised too if I was in his shoes because he didn't deserve it, but that is what is called Grace (undeserving favour). I told him, 'It is me who wrote everything and I meant every word. I am not coming to take anything from you, you can keep everything. When we meet let's be civil and greet one another and life moves on.' He must have got excited because he asked me if we could go out for dinner that night. I laughed and said, 'Not today, I am not ready yet don't push it. When I am ready we can have a coffee.'

Hard to comprehend; I had asked him for forgiveness in the letter, in-case I had done him wrong in the course of our relationship. You might ask what I was asking forgiveness for. I am neither Jesus nor a saint, and I will never be, but why did Jesus go on the cross when He was righteous? He did it for each and every one of us to have the freedom we have today—that is, if you believe. Throughout the years, I had learnt a revelation from Papa that

Chapter Seven: Immigration Revisited

forgiveness is not about the other person, it's about you, the one who needs freedom, and I live by this to today.

Until today, Saul has never said he was sorry for all he did, not that I am waiting for it. So, if I had not done it, I would be still be in bondage and waiting for him to say he was sorry. I would have probably been messing up relationships with other men, thinking they were all the same and so on. That is not the life I would have hoped for. Where I am today and the joyful person that I am today would not have happened if I had not taken the first step. If I was still holding onto my grudges I would not have opened my heart to the amazing man I met later on.

When I received the second promotion at work, I was used to working in the warehouse unloading containers. Now, I progressed up into the office as an administrator. Talk about God starting to turn things around for my good. I was used to wearing the orange polo t-shirt and steel boots at work; with the promotion came dressing up like an office lady. One day, I said to myself, 'It would be nice if I could go shopping for a few tops since I am now an office girl.' That very night, I had a dream of so many clothes being given to me and *I kid you not*, that Saturday when I went for my cleaning job, Nicky's daughter had put out all her old clothes to take to Salvos. So, she asked her mum to ask me to take anything I wanted from the piles of clothes before they gave them away to charity. Until today, I testify to this everywhere because I cannot get enough of what happened on this day—by the way, this girl happens to be a supermodel. So, you can imagine it was not just ordinary *Valleygirl* and *Tempt* clothes. The clothes were of high quality and some still had price tags. I took home more than five baskets of clothes and they all fit me perfectly. I was thinking of my young sisters and how they would each get a basket, but they are all bigger and taller than me, all the clothes were made to fit me perfectly.

Not bragging here, but I am just trying to give you a snippet of how my life has turned around. My wardrobe is one of a kind; thanks to the supermodel's generosity, I can wear my clothes for two to three years without repeating, that's how many clothes I have! And working for a shoe company does also help—I have a few hundred pairs of shoes. So why am I saying this? I didn't need to go for a face lift, or implants, or do anything to change my appearance or who I was before to prove a point or be accepted. God himself brought opportunities my way and did a makeover.

I remember in 2014 during the Christmas lunch at work the company director said to me, 'As for you we all know where your money goes'. I had to laugh, because everyone thinks I am a shopaholic. I have had so many girls befriend me and ask me to go shopping with them and then they realise that I am the worst, most boring shopping buddy. Then the question comes: 'Where do you buy all your clothes from?' I am not embarrassed to say, from charity.

As mentioned previously, I never thought I looked beautiful from a very young age, as I was tormented by most people because of my big nose and ears. According to everyone, I never smiled or laughed during my relationship years, taking pictures was the worst. God transformed all that, not makeup or *contouring* as they call it nowadays. Now you cannot tell me to stop smiling or laughing. Every now and then my boss will enter the office and ask me why I am smiling. I just can't help it, I am happy. I take a selfie almost every single day of my life now because I am grateful to be alive. I don't wear makeup; only when I have some time to spare, which is unusual, but I feel like the most beautiful girl in the world. My husband doesn't need to tell me I look gorgeous because I feel it inside. What is on the outside is a reflection of how I feel inside. Being an African girl, my hairstyle changes every other day and my husband at times is not fond of those styles. Do I care about that? No, I don't, because inside I feel beautiful and I look at myself and see a gorgeous girl, and that's all that matters.

As time passed, I met Saul one afternoon at the service station in my new car, and the surprise on his face was great. Whilst I was working in the warehouse he was used to seeing me wear the orange t-shirt, but on this particular day I was dressed to kill. Can you guess what he asked me? He asked where I was coming from. Of all the questions, this. 'Hahaha of course work,' I responded, not forgetting to mention I had been promoted into the office. I went on to fill my car, so did he, and thereafter we went on our businesses. That was the last

Chapter Seven: Immigration Revisited

time I saw him face to face. Bless the Lord!

I would still do the same thing today and ask him to forgive me. So if I may ask you, has anyone wronged you so badly that you can't stand them? Are you really waiting for them to ask for your mercy and forgiveness for whatever they did wrong? What if they move to a new country or continent—worse more, what if they die and they never get that opportunity? Are you still going to hold it against them and not move on with your life? Saul actually moved to Melbourne because all this drama had been too much for him. Who should have moved, really?

I have always been a dreamer for as long as I can remember, but I never took my dreams seriously until after the conference. I dreamt of Pastor Robert Kayanja on the 2nd of November 2010 and this was the dream:

I dreamt we were in a house with my pastors, their children, Pastor Robert and Saul. Saul was crying that he didn't have a job and that his life was messed up. Pastor Robert told him that someone in his family was causing all this trouble for him but because of his own stupidity he was making it worse. He was shown the blinds on a window and it showed the sunshine rays in-between. The sunshine rays meant there was hope for him and life wasn't as pitch dark as he thought. He was told that a man cannot lie and gossip like a woman because he had become the best and that whatever happened in his relationship was between him and his spouse only, and not for him to share with the rest of the world. This dream was beyond real, and I asked Pastor Robert if he had anything to say about me and he said nothing. And then a son appeared who happened to look exactly like Saul, and he was explaining that he had gone somewhere and the baby took weed. And the answer was his stupidity.

It was one of those dreams that leaves a deep impression, and I woke up and wrote the dream down and finished with these words, 'Thank you Lord for speaking to me. I don't know if I have to tell him or not.' It's my prayer that he can find that ray of sunshine wherever he can find it.

For some reason, I felt differently about this dream. It felt so real and now, years later, I can testify that I am Tinashe (female version of Joseph in the bible) of this time. This to me was a confirmation that I could not save Saul, he has to also save himself from his demons. He has to ask for help himself, look back at his life and see where that anger comes from.

God speaks to me through dreams and it has been an amazing journey, I should say. To dream things and see them come to pass, that was like me and God getting to know and trust one another. Or rather, me having confidence in myself, and walking with my head high. Ninety per cent of the questions I ask God in prayer before bed will be revealed by Him in a dream or vision. At times it's not straightforward—they are parables—but at the end I get it.

A year or two passed and I knew that God had forgiven me all of my past wrong choices—sex before marriage, living with a man unmarried and the pregnancy terminations. But for some reason I would still not pass through the road where the clinic was where I had the surgeries. A few times, when someone preached about abortion, I really felt condemned. So I kept asking myself why I would feel like this even when I had no regrets over my decisions. I came to realise that not all preachers or people speak under Grace and that I had to forgive myself.

One night I had a dream:

I was sleeping in my bedroom when I had a vision of Jesus in all His Glory visiting me. He asked me to be upright and to look in the mirror. Eventually I stared at myself in the mirror and saw how beautiful I was without any blemishes, and my roof just opened and this fluffy pure white, like snow, was just falling on me and the place I was standing in was just pure white, then instantly a thought of the scripture that says your sins will be washed as snow came to mind.

Isaiah 1:18 says '"Come now, let us settle the matter," says the Lord. "Though your sins are like scarlet, they shall be as white as snow; though they are red as crimson, they shall be like wool."' From my faith, all I can say is what a

Chapter Seven: Immigration Revisited

mighty God I serve. People, including the servants of God could crucify me for my past, but I constantly remind myself that there is one greater than them who washes every imperfection in me. One who does not remind me of my past to discourage me. I can listen to someone talk about abortion all day and won't even flinch. That night it was all done, He took all my condemnations and convictions. Who else can tell me otherwise when God is happy with me? There is a scripture in Acts 10:14–16 that says, '"No, Lord!" Peter answered, "I have never eaten anything impure or unclean." The voice spoke to him a second time: "Do not call anything impure" that God has made clean. This happened three times, and all at once the sheet was taken back up into heaven … ' I also learnt to forgive myself because this was something I could only imagine happening elsewhere, in a movie possibly, but to have Jesus in my bedroom for me, there was and is nothing greater than this.

Chapter Eight

FORGIVENESS AND FREEDOM

Times will change for the better when you change

—Maxwell Maltz

CHAPTER EIGHT

FORGIVENESS AND FREEDOM

By 2014 all my visa issues had been sorted out. I was an Australian Citizen; a born-again Christian, spirit-filled; a university student, working full time—and so in love with my boyfriend (my husband now). My life was more than perfect, everything was in order and God was doing miracles and wonders in my life. But one thing that I could not stand was being in the company of my old housemates. The world was now very small and I would occasionally meet my old housemates at different events. Even their phone calls annoyed me. At times, I picked up or would return missed calls in my own time, but not gladly. Our church hosted a conference and as a worship leader, I was in the forefront. After ministering a powerful worship, the preacher told me in front of everyone that I needed to forgive someone.

'Forgiveness. It's one of the greatest gifts you can give yourself, to forgive. Forgive everybody. You are relieved of carrying that burden of resentment. You really are lighter. You feel lighter. You just drop that.' (Maya Angelou)

[1]"I always love Aha! Moments, when somebody says something that made us look at life in a completely new way. When I first heard that, I literally got goose bumps. The message that came through so clearly and stayed with me is this: Forgive, so you can truly live. Forgiveness is letting go, so the past does not hold you prisoner, does not hold you hostage. One of my favourite quotes is, 'Unforgiveness unchecked becomes a cancer of the soul. What I know is that forgiveness is like medicine—medicine that can heal your pain. It can bring you peace. Forgiveness is something that you do for yourself. Forgiveness means that what someone did is no longer going to affect how you live in the present moment. When I got that, it took me to the next level of being a better person' (Oprah Winfrey).

---

[1] Ophrah Winfrey. What Oprah knows about forgiveness. June 26, 2017. http://healthylivingmadesimple.com/what-oprah-knows-about-forgiveness/

Chapter Eight: Forgiveness and Freedom

Matthew 5:23–24 says 'therefore if you are offering your gift at the altar and there you remember that your brother or sister has something against you, leave your gift there in front of the altar. First go and be reconciled to them, then come and offer your gift'. Could this scripture be more accurate? Forgiveness is very important to us all and it's a two-way thing. This scripture to me personally, just shows the importance of forgiveness for everyone regardless of who you are and how important you might think you are. No matter how powerful my worship singing was before God, I needed to forgive first before everything else. How sad would it be for me to be so anointed and use my gift to transform others, yet I myself stay in the same place of misery and probably miss heaven?

The Lord's Prayer says, 'Forgive us of our trespasses even as we forgive those who trespass against us'. This prayer is said worldwide, but people do not meditate on the words they are saying—they are powerful. I want to be that person who does unto people as I want them to do unto me in return.

I was ashamed, but as soon as the preacher said it, I just knew who he was talking about. I looked at Mama with embarrassment and soon after the service, she asked me who it was and I just said, 'My ex-housemates.' This was eight years after the student visa cancellation. I could have pretended to forget and move on with my life, but only God knew the anger and hatred I had for them. I used to think that had it not been for them I wouldn't have been as worse off as I was. *Out of sight, out of mind* is not forgiveness. And to be honest, if the Man of God hadn't mentioned it, I would have kept going and not even thought of it.

Instead of being too spiritual by fasting and praying for that day I decided to face my last fear in this chapter of my life. I knew I just had to act and not prolong this anymore as I was holding my blessings and probably theirs too. The Lord gave me a scripture in Matthew 7:1 that says, '"Do not judge, or you too will be judged.[2] For in the same way you judge others, you will be judged, and with the measure you use, it will be measured to you.[3] Why do you look at the speck of sawdust in your brother's eye and pay no attention to the plank in your own eye?[4] How can you say to your brother, 'Let me take the speck out of your eye,' when all the time there is a plank in your own eye?[5] You hypocrite, first take the plank out of your own eye, and then you will see clearly to remove the speck from your brother's eye.'"

God has a good sense of humour, if I may be so bold to say. I was amazed at this scripture because it rebuked me and I laughed for a few minutes. I was no holier than them regardless of what I assumed they did to me, causing my student visa cancellation. Until this day, I always held them responsible for the visa cancellation because of their withholding mail that should have alerted me of the consultation with the dean of college. I believe that it was their responsibility because had they passed on the letter to me I would have gone to school and sorted out the issue.

I remember when I went to see the dean he said, 'I am sorry it has to come to this, we tried to contact you with no avail. I wanted to know if you were having any difficulties in a particular subject and if we could find any solutions to help you in the next semester to pass this unit as this is your core subject. But your ignorance caused us to take further actions.' I could be wrong here, but with all this evidence I could only conclude it was them.

The scripture in Matthew that was deposited into my spirit gave me strength and courage to face my fear. I am happy to say we have all reconciled and I asked for forgiveness. Malcom X once said, 'You can't separate peace from freedom because no one can be at peace unless he has his freedom'. I was happy, free and at peace with myself. I can undoubtedly say I have forgiven and moved on. To me, this was the last chapter that needed to be finished and filed away.

I can affirm that from that day we meet occasionally, I can do anything for them without thinking twice. We are there for each other in good and bad. I have seen growth and change in them, I pray for them and I love them so much. Every time they visit me and we pray together I just cry with joy because I know that only God can heal the broken hearted and bring together what humans cannot. But here we are now, closer than before, and all I can say is victory belongs to God.

Chapter Nine

CATEGORIES OF VIOLENCE/ABUSE

CHAPTER NINE

CATEGORIES OF VIOLENCE/ABUSE

According to the Australian Bureau of Statics, in *Defining the Data Challenge for Family, Domestic and Sexual Violence, 2013*, the nine types of categories of violence are:

1. Physical
2. Sexual
3. Emotional/Psychological
4. Cultural/Spiritual
5. Financial/Economic
6. Verbal
7. Social
8. Stalking
9. Technology Facilitated Abuse.

In Australia, domestic violence is defined by the *Family Law Act 1975*[1][2] as 'violent, threatening or other behaviour by a person that coerces or controls a member of the person's family, or causes the family member to be fearful'. Firstly, are you in an abusive relationship? Or is your friend or loved one going through an abusive relationship? Or could it be you are the abuser or abused? Can you relate to my life story? I am constantly surrounded by abused women and men, so I came up with a few questions to ask the reader for a self-check of which I have been through all this.

Chapter Nine: Categories of Violence/Abuse

1. Are you constantly accused of cheating by your spouse, even though you are innocent? If you are innocent, like I was, I can guarantee that it is either he/she who is cheating on you or has cheated on you previously, or that it is just jealousy and a desire to control you.

2. Are you being beaten, punched or smacked?

3. Are you being forced to always be by his/her side during outings?

4. Does he/she always say nasty things to you and tell you it's a practical joke?

5. Does he/she ring you a thousand times a day and expect you to pick up the phone, even when he/she knows for sure that you are at work, school or home?

6. Is the insecurity in your relationship causing you anxiety?

7. Are you finding yourself losing your appetite, peace, smile or joy because of the stress in the relationship and uneasiness?

8. Are you constantly sick? (Having migraines, loss of appetite, having negative feelings etcetera.)

9. Are you now in a situation where your close family and friends are distant from you because he/she talks negative things about them even an issue that is not important he makes it bigger, and you lose that connection with family and friends?

10. Does he/she stand too close when you are on the phone or the computer, watching your every movement?

11. Do they force you to have sex with them? (This is rape.)

12. Does he/she show up unnecessarily at places you are or even at midnight or the early hours of the morning? Do you think you're his/her very own world?

13. Does he/she complain that you spend too much doing your hobbies or, in my case, spending too much time at church?

14. Does he/she accuse you of spending too much time with his/her relatives and remind you that it's because of him/her that you even know these people?

15. Has he/she come and confessed to your family and friends that they would not do it again, but the very minute/day you leave those people they still behave the same? One thing I know is that a leopard does not change his spots, so *wake up honey*.

16. Has he/she stripped you naked in front of people or humiliated you?

17. Is he/she constantly reminding you of the things they have done/helped you with? Do they remind you that you wouldn't be where you are now had it not been for them?

If you can relate to me, what is stopping you from leaving this abuser? Is it the fear of the unknown? I want to encourage you to take a step today because whichever way you look at it, you're already dead, it is just a matter of time or day when you will be physically killed. There are so many organisations to ring, such as: *Crisis Care*, which is 'a telephone information and counselling service for people in crisis needing urgent help'.

Nowadays, spouses even take revenge using kids to taunt their partners by killing the innocent children. God has given you another day—which is today—to seize this moment and make a plan to leave, today, tomorrow, on the weekend or in a few weeks' time, but *do not prolong the process*.

You have to be wise with your plans if you are leaving a violent partner. I had to come up with an exit plan because when you eventually tell them you are leaving, not only does it surprise them but it puts them in an uncomfortable place. **PLAN YOUR EXIT FIRST AND THEN EXECUTE IT!!!** If anything is to go wrong, when you're prepared, the chances of dying are low. Things did not go according to my plan, I was hurt but I am still alive today.

Chapter Nine: Categories of Violence/Abuse

LESSONS I LEARNT FROM THE YEARS OF ABUSE

There has never been a meaningful life built on easy street
—John Paul Warren

- I don't play the blame game. Every decision I made had its own consequences, whether good or bad, so I stand by the decisions I made.

- I don't know everything. When in doubt or not sure, ask for help. I thought I knew what I was doing, but now when I look back I didn't know anything, I was just going by experience on what I saw growing up.

- I am not a slave to my African culture, tradition or religion, therefore I ought to do what is best for me before these things. I choose to be the change I want to see, as a person who now knows what is right and wrong.

- I learnt that there are so many things that need to be changed in the African culture or tradition, as some things are not relevant today. What could have worked a few years ago cannot work in today's society—times are changing. The New South Wales (NSW) Assistant Police Commissioner Mark Murdoch 2013 said of domestic and family violence as a gendered issue, 'men need to wake up to the fact that it is a men's problem … until they wake up to that fact, nothing's going to change'.

- Staying too long in this abusive relationship had its ramifications. I did not realise this then, but when I was desperate for help in the midst of being abused, I ended up abusing myself to take away the pain, and because I was numb to pain I began to hurt myself. The suicidal thoughts began to occur to me at some point. I starved myself without even realising and started thinking of how I could take revenge. I began to do things that were very much out of character. Now, when I look back, I was probably going mental or crazy without realising it.

According to the research done by Kavito Alejo, 'Domestic violence can cause a number of short- and long-term physical and mental health problems. Some of the physical injuries that can occur include cuts, bruises, bite marks, concussions, broken bones, penetrative injuries such as knife wounds, miscarriages, joint damage, loss of hearing and vision, migraines, permanent disfigurement, arthritis, hypertension, heart disease, and sexually transmitted infections including human papillomavirus, which can lead to cervical cancer and eventually death. Some of the mental health problems that can occur from domestic violence include depression, alcohol or substance abuse, anxiety, personality disorders, posttraumatic stress disorder, sleeping and eating disorders, social dysfunction, and suicide'.

Chapter Nine: Categories of Violence/Abuse

- Communication is the key to every relationship. The culture I grew up in constrained me, but now when I am wronged I speak my mind, literally. In the book *I know why the caged bird sings*, Maya Angelou said, 'Now no one is going to make you talk, possibly no one can. But bear in mind, language is man's way of communicating with his fellow man and it is language alone which separates him from the lower animals.'

- Racism is a subject that needs to be discussed by parents when they send their children away to foreign countries. It is naïve for parents to think that their children are going to a land of milk and honey. Without any experience or knowledge, the struggle is much more difficult.

- It is my duty as a human being to, when given the opportunity, speak of my experiences without shame or trying to hide so I can also help those who are not aware.

- It's not only your close family and friends that can help you. At times they also don't know how to. Use all the channels you can find. With the world of social media, I see and follow people who inspire me. For example, when I needed clarification on publishing I went to Nkandu Beltz. When I needed help on how to start raising awareness I went to Ebro Kebe and contacted the Minister of Domestic violence and abuse. When I need clarification on an issue I find the person who is qualified in that area.

- My culture did not prepare me to think critically when I was confronted with these problems of domestic violence and abuse. I didn't even know what to do or say. That is why I have made it my mission to speak out.

COULD I HAVE DONE THINGS DIFFERENTLY WITH THE KNOWLEDGE I HAVE NOW?

With what I know now, I should have just left him when he mistreated me the first time and never looked back. When I went to see the lawyer in Subiaco I should have just bit the bullet and left Saul. I was still waiting for the people who were close to me to approve and help me; they did in their own way, but that just prolonged my suffering. We can't all be experts in everything; there are people qualified for domestic and violence issues, who could have assisted me more in this particular case, but I was more comfortable with what I knew.

With my upbringing, I fed off the approval of the elders in everything I did, I danced to their right and left. In this relationship, I needed someone to just tell me to leave him and give me that assurance that I would be okay, even if it meant going back to Zimbabwe. But I didn't get that. Nicky told me that two years into the suffering, but I was still scared. Saul saw that weakness in me and exploited it to his advantage.

In the beginning, I should have reported him to the police, period!

I shouldn't have taken him back the many times I did knowing we had not sought professional help. I just gave us time to cool down after arguments and did not actually sort out the real cause of the arguments.

Chapter Nine: Categories of Violence/Abuse

HOW MUCH STRONGER HAVE I BECOME?

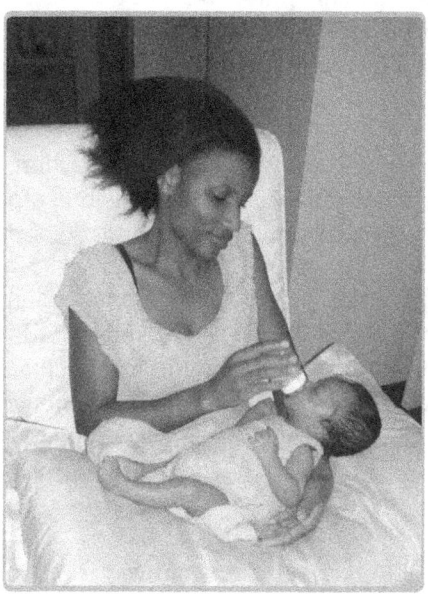

I have had hindrances in publishing this book from the people I felt would understand me and this story. I will not lie, I was hurt to the core. I had to get off social media and could not sleep. However, I got to the place where I told myself, they might not get me but if a life is saved, I have done my part in this world. No one can stop me, not even my husband. I am no longer a person who seeks another person's approval when I think I am doing the right thing.

When I entered my current relationship, which was nine years ago, on the first date I aired out every expectation so that I would not get any surprises. I talked about everything, literally, which has brought out this new confident and strong woman I am today. I even asked how he behaved when he is upset.

The fact that I can now share my story with the whole world shows how I have grown and matured as a person.

I went from burning with rage to forgiveness and to living a life of joy in abundance. As I mentioned previously, I still have friends to this very day who despise Saul, and it is my prayer that they too can forgive him because, through my experience, God knows each and every person's heart. Anyone who knows or has met me knows I am very happy. So, this is not a pretence, this happiness; I have gone through the emotions and then let it all go.

The fact that I understand that people who have hurt me have their own versions of the story and that they have a responsibility to work on themselves shows maturity. They are accountable for their actions, as I am too.

Having overcome my battles with my ex-housemates and Saul I thought there could be no greater tests than these, as I would die. I have faced even more challenges since then and I am still being tested, but that is life. In fact, when I look back at where I have come from I find hope in the battles I face today. The scripture in Luke 12:48 says, 'From everyone to whom much has been given, much will be required; and to whom they entrusted much, of him they will ask all the more'.

I can testify that I am stronger, as I don't run away from troubles as I did before. For example, since being a worship leader, I have been put in the spotlight and a few married male pastors have tested my faith by being flirtatious, and it really put me down. I remember an incident where I was so overwhelmed I got sick to the point of vomiting, which was a first with my migraines, and the last. Here I was, trying not to be rude, and at the same time the behaviour was contradicting their positions and putting me in an awkward position. With my previous behaviour, it could have been so easy to stop going to church and keep to myself, as people I trust let me down. However, I always remind myself they are human, like me, and full of weaknesses too. That being said, I do not keep the conversation quiet, I talk about these things publicly to bring awareness so that people in power do not abuse their leadership.

The greatest test to this day is of my husband being a non-believer and not of African descent as myself. This has tested me beyond my imagination. I thought I was calm (well he is much calmer than me), that loving each

Chapter Nine: Categories of Violence/Abuse

other was a piece of cake and probably what I needed, coming from an abusive relationship. As a couple, we are comfortable around one another and it never crossed my mind that not all the extended families and even some of my fellowship members would not be thrilled with our relationship. The fact that we have become aware, honest with our emotions and use open communication has made us stronger. The scripture that says, 'For we wrestle not against flesh and blood, but against principalities, against powers, against the rulers of the darkness of this world, against spiritual wickedness in high places …' (Ephesians, 6:12) gives me strength. I now know that there are some battles to fight, but this one is definitely not for me to fight, because not even bleaching my skin or getting a straight wave will help. A few people hating me cannot be compared to the love I have received from my very many friends and families. I am not losing anything—those who hate are the ones who lose.

Last year, I went through an emotional period, to the point of almost breaking down. I had talked myself into how I would solve the dowry process when the time came but I could never have imagined what was before me. No matter how I prepared myself mentally, I soon realised that I live with people and in order to get to that mutual understanding, people need to talk. Keeping quiet has never solved problems, I should have learnt that by now. My husband now had asked my parents for my hand in marriage and we had planned on the dowry process and everything that goes in between. Concurrently, we had already started building a house when all this was happening, so when the house was ready, we moved in together before the dowry was settled. This was contrary to my wish and the complications of mixed marriage just messed me up. After a few days of crying myself to sleep I had a beautiful dream:

I had gone to the shops with my friends to look for print materials in particular. Whilst walking around the shop I liked a material and put it on my shoulder. We continued to look through all other materials and we didn't buy anything but I accidentally left the shop with the material on my shoulder. When we reached the exit door of the shopping centre I realised I had this material on my shoulder and so I told my friends that we needed to go back to the shop. As we returned to the shop we were met by the security guards who were coming after me and I told them what had happened, but they were not having any of my excuses and handcuffed me. As we were having an argument, one of my friends who turned out to be me, but frail looking, sick and with sores all over, said it was her who had done it. For some reason, we happened to know that she didn't have long to live and we felt sorry for her. I started arguing with her and asking her what was wrong with her and telling her that she shouldn't take the blame for my own mistake. She insisted it was her and security took her with them in handcuffs, and I was in shock because this girl was exactly me but in a frail state.

Parables are not only in the Bible; even today, God still uses parables. The dream reminded me that God takes our place in situations that we cannot bear. 1 Peter 2:24 states that 'He himself bore our sins in his body on the cross, so that we might die to sins and live for righteousness, by His wounds you have been healed'. After this dream I felt peace, and I just knew that God was in control. I decided to cast this burden of dowry pressure and living situation to God, and within four months the dowry was paid and I was at peace, not to mention that I am now happily married.

My personal opinion on dowry as an ongoing tradition is that it should be abolished or deconstructed. In the old times, people gave away cattle and livestock. The meaning was just simple acceptance of two families joining together. However, in these times where money is king, people have put money before their morals. You cannot put a figure on a human being; no matter how much we try to explain that it is not selling a person, payment of dowry insinuates an enslaving mentality amongst African men. In the old times there were no engagement rings (honestly speaking, what girl wouldn't want a sparkler on her finger?), so how do we expect the men to buy an engagement ring, pay dowry and prepare for a wedding? The new couple will still need furniture for the new home; are we, as people, not putting a financial burden on newlyweds before they settle into marriage?

So, my dear friends, forgiveness is the key to living a free life. Once you are set free you are free indeed—you can enter any door without limitations. There is no stress of whether you will meet that person and hide away, you walk with your head high. Romans 12:19 says 'Do not take revenge, my dear friends, but leave room for God's wrath, for it is written: "It is mine to avenge; I will repay," says the Lord.' If I had revenged those who have hurt me I would be in prison right now, if not dead. I would have hurt so many families and would not be married to the wonderful man I have. I would not have seen the beauty of this world and others.

Chapter Ten

MY NEW RELATIONSHIP

Harry was waiting patiently while his wife talked to friends. I feel like the Mona Lisa's frame. No one pays the least attention to me, but I get to hold and support one of the world's most beautiful women. Actually, that frame is pretty special, too. It's a gift, made a century ago from the Comtessse de Behague. Of course, people viewing the two together will tend to focus on the picture, but the painting and frame add value to each other, they depend on each other just like a good marriage.

— Elizabeth Gozney

CHAPTER TEN

MY NEW RELATIONSHIP

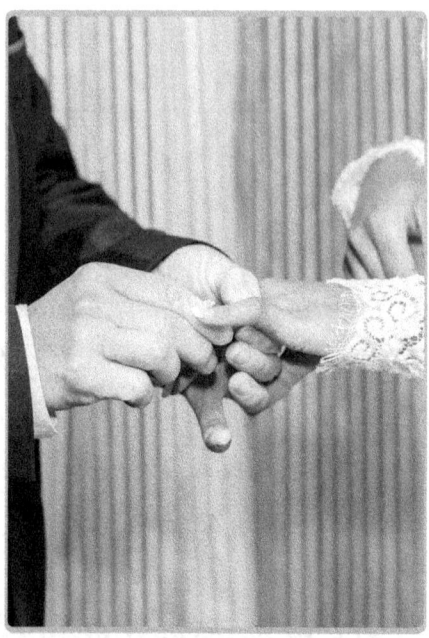

I have been mentioning and giving examples of my husband Danny throughout the book. I feel like I am living in heaven on earth. We are different in every way possible, however, in those differences we complement one another. Danny has been supporting me and encouraging me to write this book, which shows how much he supports my work and passions.

Not only do he and I communicate openly, but we have learnt to recognise how we behave when upset. For example, when my husband is annoyed about anything he usually plays golf or just keeps quiet until he cools down and starts over anew and he is okay. On the other hand, I want to talk about what

Chapter Ten: My New Relationship

has happened and sort it out there and then. Over time, I learnt his way of conduct is better because when you are highly agitated you can say anything. Better to walk away and refresh; it is not easy, but it can be done. Laurence J. Peter said, 'Speak when you angry, and you will make the best speech you'll ever regret.' This has helped us in our relationship for the past nine years, to know when not to cross the boundaries. With my Taekwondo skills, he wouldn't dare touch me unless he wants to die. I am just kidding—he has never abused me.

I go to church (as I will) and practise everything about my faith; in our house, I have a prayer room and I pay my tithes faithfully and pray without any problem whatsoever. We communicate about everything and we understand one another—for all I know, God is love. I am encouraging people to not be quick to judge and think that people who are different from you are not good and the ones who are similar are good. Labelling other people is not good in society. God has revealed so much about my marriage; had it not been for the Lord, we would not have made it this far, with people pointing out how different we are.

Because I am a worship leader, some of my fellow brethren have told me personally of how they do not approve of my husband. But when I look at their marriages, I am in a way better position to testify to the goodness of marriage than they are. One guy openly said, 'I am not happy with this fella. Have the pastors and your parents met this guy?' I could not believe that he could have the guts to comment on my relationship when he had not even met the 'guy' he disliked. So, I encourage anyone who is happy and has good communication with their better half not to let petty issues or concerns of the outside world hinder them from their blessing.

Who said a woman's place is in the kitchen? In our house, whoever gets home first prepares dinner—after all, we all have to eat, right? If I am unwell or tired I am very much encouraged to take a nap and rest, and there is nothing wrong with that and neither does that mean I am lazy. Danny is an early riser; from Monday to Sunday he wakes up at 4.30 am. Unless there is something wrong in my head there is no way I would wake up that early to make breakfast because I am a wife. We acknowledge that we are different and ought to respect one another, which is healthy. If I followed my culture, I would have to wake up and cook breakfast and sort out his work clothing, yet my body cannot handle the lack of sleep. Marriages and relationships are a great thing and need to be celebrated, if only people can stop following tradition and do what works for their household.

Chapter Eleven

WAS EVERYTHING ALL DOOM AND GLOOM?

She was unstoppable. Not because she didn't have failures or doubts, but because she continued on despite them

— Beau Taplin

CHAPTER ELEVEN

WAS EVERYTHING ALL DOOM AND GLOOM?

I was in this violent and abusive relationship and I had stopped going to university even after I was put on the spouse visa, thinking *I will get in the right mindset* and I never did, till I decided to quit the relationship. However, great things happened to me as well. As Nelson Mandela once said, 'We can all do more to reach out, take care, and serve the well-being of others. No difficulty, problem or breakdown need stop you from choosing and living a life of service.' First and Foremost, meeting the Mpofu and Serugga families was a miracle. These two families embraced me like their own child, sister or friend and I acknowledged that from the beginning. I felt and still feel at home in their presence.

When I had to run away from Saul at times, it was relieving to know there were people I could call and who would rescue me 24/7. These families opened their doors and homes to me so that I could have a place to sleep and

Chapter Eleven: Was Everything All Doom And Gloom?

stay for a while, otherwise I could have become homeless so easily. It was always one of them or the other, that acknowledged the good things about me that made me realise that even though I didn't know what to do, I was a good person. Had it not been for these two families who kept reminding me that I was a good person, I would have given up on life so many times.

When I went home in 2011 and told Aunty Maggie about these two families, she said to me, 'It's not only about these people being good to you. Had you not been the kind, giving, humble and good person you are, they would not have been willing to help you.' I don't ever remember being rude to them; because of my circumstances I was grateful and thoughtful in my responses.

Regardless of all the troubles I faced whilst still in a relationship with Saul, I still worked full time. The times I stayed with Mama and Papa, Papa at times would lend me a car to drive to work because I was so determined to be better, even though it was so easy to stay in bed and cry my sorrows away. I enjoyed working at Sealanes, my first full-time workplace in Australia. I still looked forward to every morning or evening when I went to work because the gents I worked with were awesome human beings. In hindsight, that is why I never hated all other males, because all the other males around me respected me.

I spent so much time with Mama and Papa and their children that before I knew it, I was the first-born child of the family. Wherever Mama and Papa went I was there, be it meetings with elders in the community, church leaders, parties or weddings. I soon learnt to be of service to humanity in any way I could. I cooked and ushered for so many wedding ceremonies and engagements in Perth that it came to a time where I told myself *if I am not invited to be a guest I am not attending*. That is how many I attended and offered my help for no payment. I was helping Mama and Papa with their ministering work before they became Official Pastors, so that I soon regained my love for singing. I had lost the Tweetbird in me during the years of being subjected to domestic violence and abuse.

I got my passion back for music, because Mama and Papa are music lovers too. Now the whole family is full of musicians. We would sing, dance and watch movies most weekends if we were not helping churches to establish themselves. I enjoyed being part of helping others in any way I could. Now I am not surprised by the passion I have for helping anyone in difficulty.

It was through Mama's work with Doula (someone who offers emotional and physical support to a woman and her partner before, during and after childbirth) that she helped me to overcome my fears of holding newborns. I remember one evening going to a Doula conference and I had to watch videos of newborn babies. I cried. I was traumatised, but we took it one day at a time. The more newborns we went to visit the better I got, and now I have no problem whatsoever, that love I had for babies when I was young has come back.

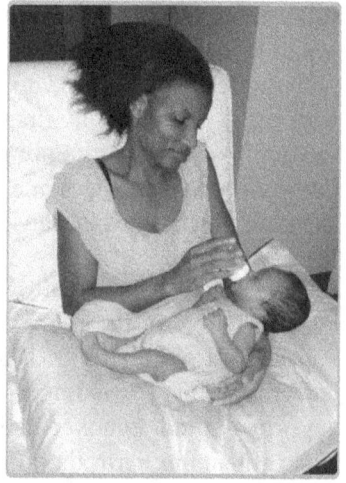

Mama used to call me her profit/asset and complimented me on my looks and clothing. I soon gained some confidence in myself, in knowing I am beautiful the way I am. From the first time I met Kiri when I had just arrived in Australia in 2004 till today, she has teased me and called me *musalad*, a nickname for snobs in Zimbabwe. To some this would be a good compliment but with all that I was going through with my relationship with Saul, it was difficult to find the goodness in me because I was constantly being put down. Kiri was actually the first African woman friend I made in Perth.

Nicky, might be a White Kenyan, but she is one of the most humble and classy women I have ever met. I have learnt a lot from her and I can never get enough of her. When I grow up I want to be like her. She is the one who said enough was enough and opened my eyes to the world I could never imagine. That step of faith was enough to give me the hope that I could live a life free of violence and abuse.

Chapter Eleven: Was Everything All Doom And Gloom?

When Missy Trish came into my life in 2007 it was like a hurricane that hit me. My life went into overdrive; she is one girl who is full of life and joy. Before I knew what hit me, I was a ray of sunshine. She would not allow me to have a bad day. We did everything any young independent girls can do with dignity. Nothing was too expensive and nothing couldn't be done or accomplished. We never drank but we were too joyful; every day and moment spent with Missy Trish was heaven to me. I soon went back to studying in 2009 and, as they say, the rest is history.

In a nutshell, I surrounded or found myself amongst the most positive and driven women one needs in life. And each and every one of them has brought out the diamond gem in me. Their influence on me has been nothing but positive. Each and every one of these women has influenced me in their own unique way, so you can imagine how much I have within me to download and pass on to the others. Maya Angelou would say 'If you get, give. If you learn, teach.'

All of these positive influences made me to be the woman of faith that I am today. I am not your Sunday Christian: where there is a need I am there.

GREENER PASTURES

RECOMMENDED READINGS

RECOMMENDED READINGS

1. Alejo, Kavita (2014) 'Long-Term Physical and Mental Health Effects of Domestic Violence', *Themis: Research Journal of Justice Studies and Forensic Science*: Vol. 2: Iss. 1, Article 5. http://scholarworks.sjsu.edu/themis/vol2/iss1/5

2. Belinda Clearly (2018) 'Speak even if your voice shakes': The powerful anti-bullying message Akubra girl 'Dolly', 14, wrote just days before she took her own life—and which her family hopes will save others. http://www.dailymail.co.uk/news/article-5253237/Akubra-girl-Dollys-strong-anti-bullying-message.html#ixzz53psZBIkk

3. De facto relationships http://www.familycourt.gov.au/wps/wcm/connect/fcoaweb/family-law-matters/separation-and-divorce/defacto-relationships/

4. Domestic Violence laws in Australia, 2009. https://www.dss.gov.au/sites/default/files/documents/05_2012/domestic_violence_laws_in_australia_-_june_2009.pdf

5. Female Genital Mutilation (FGM) https://www.mtholyoke.edu/~mcbri20s/classweb/worldpolitics/index.html

6. 'George Clooney reveals his lawyer wife Amal has also faced sexual harassment at work as he claims abuse is not just Hollywood's problem but rife in all industries'. http://www.dailymail.co.uk/news/article-5008567/George-Clooney-reveals-Amal-faced-sexual-harassment.html

7. 'Manipulation in Relationships – and how to deal with it'. http://lifeesteem.org/wellness/wellness_manipulation.html

8. Maya Angelou (1969), *I know why the caged bird sings*.

9. Nkandu Beltz (2014), *I Have the power. Unlocking your potential to change the world.*

10. Sindiwe Magona (1992), *Forced to Grow*

11. Scoot Shaper, Domestic Violence: The Fact Behind The Myths. https://www.blueribbonproject.org/our-programs/backpacks-of-love/about-backpacks-of-love/22-relationships/165-domestic-violence-the-fact-behind-the-myths.html

12. Bianca London, for mailonline (September 19, 2017). From one mother to another: Kate makes first appearance since her pregnancy announcement as she urges parents to teach their children how to be open about their feelings. http://www.dailymail.co.uk/femail/article-4895684/Duchess-Cambridge-stars-candid-video-message.html#ixzz56NrihPfm

13. Kate Campbell, *Perth Now* (January 7, 2018) 'Time to man up on home violence, WA's anti-domestic violence minister Simone McGurk urges'. https://www.perthnow.com.au/news/wa/time-to-man-up-on-home-violence-was-anti-domestic-violence-minister-simone-mcgurk-urges-ng-b88705904z

14. Andrea Booth (*SBS News*, 2018). 'Criminologist warns against sensationalizing Victoria's African youth crime'. https://www.sbs.com.au/news/criminologist-warns-against-sensationalising-victoria-s-african-youth-crime

To anyone in need of spiritual help I recommend:

Pastors Timothy and Peruth Serugga of Oasis Faith Church. #0402 704 466, 0422 217 850.

Pastors Robert and Gracia Mukibii of Voice of Hope International Church on 0415 063 282

24-HOUR HELPLINES IN WESTERN AUSTRALIA

If it is not an emergency and you need help, these are telephone numbers you can call 24 hours a day, seven days a week.

If you are assisting someone who does not speak English, first call the Translating and Interpreting Service (TIS) on 13 14 50 and they can connect you with the service of your choice and interpret for you.

Crisis Care Helpline is available 24 hours a day. Trained counsellors are ready to take calls at Lifeline on 13 11 14, Samaritans on 135 247 Telephone (08) 9223 1111 or free call 1800 RESPECT.

Men's Domestic Violence Helpline: Telephone (08) 9223 1199 or free call 1800 000 599.

Women's Domestic Violence Helpline (including for referral to a women's refuge): Telephone (08) 9223 1188 or free call 1800 007 339.

Sexual Assault Resource Centre: Telephone (08) 9340 1828 or free call 1800 199 888.

Police: In an emergency dial 000.

ABOUT THE AUTHOR
TINASHE ANGELINE LA

Tinashe Angeline La was born in Zimbabwe and moved to Australia at the age of 18 to continue her higher education at the University of Notre Dame. She has shown resilience and strength throughout her life journey, as written in this book. She might not have thought she had the confidence, however, overcoming all she has, she has revealed herself to be a woman who is determined to live a life she dreams of, even though she cannot see it yet. Having overcome and realised that lack of knowledge and lack of awareness was a barrier in her struggles, she has taken a stand to help others. Realising that she didn't have different sources of help was another barrier. With her determination, she had to step out of her comfort zone, which was seen as outrageous or rebellious and against the traditional norms, to get to where she wanted to be. Being surrounded by abused individuals who seem to know and not know, and seeing how many youths find it hard to open up to their surroundings regarding relationships, she hopes to initiate the conversation, *Where it is kept quiet.* Tinashe realised that her story can encourage those going through the same situation, to inspire them to face their fears and go on to live beautiful lives beyond the mountain before them. If she lived for three years in an abusive relationship, found the strength to leave, and go on to pursue her dreams, then others can do the same. In digging deep to understand why she kept quiet during the years of abuse, she looks at how her environments, such as the African culture, tradition, religion and lack of information, constrained her and the opportunities available to her in her new society.

www.ingramcontent.com/pod-product-compliance
Lightning Source LLC
Chambersburg PA
CBHW070602010526
44118CB00012B/1423